A LITERARY Paris

Hemingway, Colette, Sedaris, and Others on the UNCOMMON Lure of the City of Light

JAMIE COX ROBERTSON

Adamsmedia

AVON, MASSACHUSETTS

To Joan, ...

Copyright © 2010 by Jamie Cox Roberson
All rights reserved.

This book, or parts thereof, may not be reproduced in any form without permission from the publisher; exceptions are made for brief excerpts used in published reviews.

Published by
Adams Media, a division of F+W Media, Inc.
57 Littlefield Street, Avon, MA 02322. U.S.A.
www.adamsmedia.com

ISBN 10: 1-60550-987-6
ISBN 13: 978-1-60550-987-7
eISBN 10: 1-4405-0740-6
eISBN 13: 978-1-4405-0740-3

Printed in China.

10   9   8   7   6   5   4   3   2   1

Library of Congress Cataloging-in-Publication Data
is available from the publisher.

This publication is designed to provide accurate and authoritative information with regard to the subject matter covered. It is sold with the understanding that the publisher is not engaged in rendering legal, accounting, or other professional advice. If legal advice or other expert assistance is required, the services of a competent professional person should be sought.

—From a *Declaration of Principles* jointly adopted by a Committee of the American Bar Association and a Committee of Publishers and Associations

Many of the designations used by manufacturers and sellers to distinguish their product are claimed as trademarks. Where those designations appear in this book and Adams Media was aware of a trademark claim, the designations have been printed with initial capital letters.

This book is available at quantity discounts for bulk purchases.
For information, please call 1-800-289-0963.

Dedicated to Christopher, my loving husband and favorite traveling companion.

"If you are lucky enough to have lived in Paris as a young man, then wherever you go for the rest of your life, it stays with you, for Paris is a moveable feast." —Ernest Hemingway

"To err is human. To loaf is Parisian." —Victor Hugo

"It sounds like a paradox, but it is a very simple truth, that when today we look for American art we find it mainly in Paris. When we find it out of Paris, we at least find a good deal of Paris in it." —Henry James

"France has neither winter nor summer nor morals—apart from these drawbacks it is a fine country." —Mark Twain

Special thanks to Alison Picard, my agent, for seeing the beauty in this book from the beginning, and to Andrea Norville, my editor, for making my job so easy. Thanks also to Marie and Andrew Hartness for sharing little things about Paris that only native Parisians would know.

From *Giovanni's Room* by James Baldwin, copyright © 1956 by James Baldwin. Used by permission of Doubleday, a division of Random House, Inc.

From *Capturing Paris* by Katharine Davis. Copyright © 2006 by the author and reprinted by permission of St. Martin's Griffin, an imprint of St. Martin's Press, LLC.

From *As They Were* by M. F. K. Fisher, copyright © 1955, 1961, 1979, 1981, 1982 by M. F. K. Fisher. Used by permission of Alfred a. Knopf, a division of Random House, Inc.

"Courting Rituals of the Saint-Germain-des-Prés," from *I Wish Someone Were Waiting for Me Somewhere* by Anna Gavalda, translated by Karen L. Marker, copyright © 2003 by Penguin Group (USA) Inc. Original copyright © 1999 by Le dilettante. Used by permission of Riverhead Books, an imprint of Penguin Group (USA) Inc.

Reprinted with the permission of Scribner, a Division of Simon & Schuster, Inc. from *A Moveable Feast* by Ernest Hemingway. Copyright © 1964 by Mary Hemingway. Copyright renewed © 1992 by John H. Hemingway, Patrick Hemingway and Gregory Hemingway.

From *Satori in Paris*, reprinted by permission of SLL/Sterling Lord Literistic, Inc. Copyright © 1966 by Jack Kerouac.

From *Chasing Cézanne* by Peter Mayle, copyright © 1997 by Escargot Productions, Ltd. Used by permission of Alfred A. Knopf, a division of Random House, Inc.

From *Me Talk Pretty One Day* by David Sedaris. Copyright © 2000 by David Sedaris. By permission of Little Brown & Company.

From *April in Paris*, by Michael Wallner, translated by John Cullen, translation copyright © 2007 by John Cullen. Copyright © 2006 by Luchterhand Literaturverlag, a division of Verlagsgruppe Random House GmbH. International Rights Management: Susanna Lea Associates, Paris. Used by permission of Nan A. Talese, an imprint of The Doubleday Broadway Publishing Group, a division of Random House, Inc.

From *Our Paris* by Edmund White, copyright © 1995 by Edmund White. Used by permission of Alfred A. Knopf, a division of Random House, Inc

Unless otherwise noted, all sources are in the public domain. Thanks to Project Gutenberg, Harvard University Libraries, and Google Books for making them available.

Contents

INTRODUCTION

The first time I went to Paris I was seventeen and quite certain that I would sit in a café and write a great novel. Having just read a lot of Hemingway and Fitzgerald, and having learned enough about Gertrude Stein to be envious, I thought I might even meet some fellow aspiring writers and together we would achieve literary greatness.

Well, this didn't happen—except for the part about going to Paris and sitting in cafés. I went with friends who knew how to have fun but had no interest in writing, and I didn't meet any aspiring writers the whole time I was there. Although there was one young man, obviously American with his white tennis shoes, sitting at a corner table of an outdoor café who looked pensive while scribbling frantically in a spiral bound notebook (this was before laptops), he didn't seem to be enjoying himself, which was a shame, because there is so much in Paris to enjoy. I decided that all of those novels that I read must have been written with a fair amount of talent and a whole lot of hard work, rather than divine inspiration and good wine. But there's no denying the city's charm and the way, if you allow it, Paris can broaden your senses and open your imagination. Perhaps that's the reason why experiencing Paris is practically a literary tradition.

In *Tropic of Cancer*, Henry Miller talks about a writer's need to go to Paris. "It is no accident that propels people like us to Paris. Paris is simply an artificial stage, a revolving stage that permits the spectator to glimpse all phases of the conflict. Of itself Paris initiates no dramas. They are begun elsewhere. Paris is simply an obstetrical instrument that tears the living embryo from the womb and puts it in the incubator. Paris is the cradle of artificial births. Rocking here in the cradle each one slips back into his soil: one dreams back to Berlin, New York, Chicago, Vienna, Minsk. Vienna is never more Vienna than in Paris. Everything is raised to apotheosis. The cradle gives up its babes and new ones take their places. . . ."

I was reminded of Miller's words the first time I read Hemingway's memoir, *A Moveable Feast*, which covers his younger days in Paris. He opens the book with a scene in a Parisian café where he is trying to write his short story "Up in Michigan." It's a terrific piece proving, for him at least, that Michigan was never more Michigan than when he was in Paris.

But writers visiting the city of light also wrote about life in Paris, even if they waited until they no longer lived there.

The idea for this book was born when I began thinking about all the novels set in Paris and how each story seem to say, "This is my Paris. I may love it, I may hate it, but this is my Paris." You'll find a story about a country woman from rural France going to Paris, an ex-convict trying to rejoin Parisian society, a hip single French woman meeting a stranger with the hopes of finding love, and an undercover German soldier during the War.

These stories, all written by master storytellers, reveal a turbulent Paris, a stylish Paris, an industrious Paris and a Paris of romance and loneliness. After all, who better than Émile Zola to give us a lesson in the sophisticated yet turbulent world within Paris? Or a gifted German writer like Michael Wallner to remind us that people are people no matter the time or place? Who better than Victor Hugo to capture the political climate within the city and Anna Gavalda to remind us that love is hard to find even in the city of romance?

In the writings of these authors, you will find different takes on the same places, and similar wit in very different times. I have placed Edmund White's piece just before Zola's since they cover much of the same parts of Paris at such different times in history. I also thought it would be nice to have two of America's best humorists back to back—Mark Twain and David Sedaris. Not since Twain has an American written about Paris with such a sharp wit.

Throughout the book you will find notes about the places visited by the literary characters. Perhaps when you take this little book to Paris, you will find a café on rue Mouffetard to drink your rum St. James while watching it rain like Hemingway did, or dine at Deux Magots like everyone else, or maybe you'll find a new place right where you expected something entirely different. After all, places change. One thing that won't change, however, is the quality of these stories and the part of Paris they reveal. That will never change, and I find that comforting.

If you find yourself strolling down Saint Germain-des-Prés after reading Gavalda, you may wonder if a handsome stranger is going to ask you out to dinner, or if you get the chance to visit the Musée du Montparnasse, you may imagine the Bohemian life that Baldwin wrote about but no longer exists. Even if you never go to Paris, Hemingway makes it easy to imagine yourself walking down rue Mouffetard in the rain.

I find the scenes from great stories coming to mind when I least expect it, and that's probably the best thing about being a well-read traveler. You're never completely alone even if you appear to be dining by yourself in a Paris café.

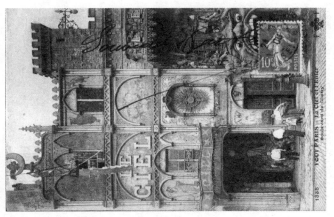

Boulevard Clichy, 1908

Giovanni's Room

BY JAMES BALDWIN (1956)

Born in 1924 in Harlem, New York, to a single mom, James Baldwin was still a boy when his mother married a Pentecostal preacher named David Baldwin. Baldwin adopted James and at fourteen James Baldwin became a minister. While in high school, however, he discovered he had a knack for writing. A turning point in his

№ 1

literary career came early on when he met writer Richard Wright who helped him secure a writer's fellowship so he could devote his time to writing and reading literature. In 1948, Baldwin moved to Paris where he was able to live more comfortably with his skin color and his homosexuality while dedicating his time to writing. He became famous with his first book, *Go Tell It on the Mountain*. After nine years in Paris, he returned to an America in the midst of a Civil Rights Movement and was outraged by what he witnessed. He wrote three books of essays dedicated to the topic: *Nobody Knows My Name* (1961), *The Fire Next Time* (1963), and *More Notes of a Native Son*.

Eventually Baldwin returned to France and lived there for the remainder of his life. Over time, the people of France came to consider him one of their own and named him Commander of the Legion of Honor in 1986. He died one year later in Saint-Paul-de-Vance. His body was returned to the United States and he was buried in Harlem.

Much of Baldwin's work deals with racism and personal exploration. His stories were written in a personable, friend-to-friend manner and he chose his words carefully in order to ignite the reaction he wanted from his readers—usually shock and action. The language he used, no matter the genre, was both powerful and eloquent. Even if the subject was ugly, his words were beautiful and written with the elegance of great poetry and an uncommon fluidity.

Giovanni's Room was Baldwin's second novel and largely controversial because of its homoeroticism. In *Giovanni's Room*, Baldwin's Paris is both gritty and breathtaking. Set in Paris post–World War II, David, both the narrator and main character, keeps company with the Saint Germain gay crowd and falls in love with a young Italian bartender named Giovanni. David is also engaged to an American girl at this time in an effort to squash his unwanted sexual desires. Giovanni, however, proves to be too great a temptation and they quickly become lovers. This scene has one of the novel's many spot-on and memorable descriptions of Paris.

FROM CHAPTER THREE

At five o'clock in the morning Guillaume locked the door of the bar behind us. The streets were empty and grey. On a corner near the bar a butcher had already opened his shop and one could see him within, already bloody, hacking at the meat. One of the great, green Paris buses lumbered past, nearly empty, its bright electric flag waving fiercely to indicate a turn. A *garçon de café* spilled water on the sidewalk before his establishment and swept it into the gutter. At the end of a long, curving street which faced us were the trees of the boulevard and straw chairs piled high before cafes and the great magnificent spire, as Hella and I believed, in Paris. The street beyond the *place* stretched before us to the river and, hidden beside and behind us, meandered to Montparnasse.

MONTPARNASSE

Located on the Left Bank along the Seine River, Montparnasse became a popular gathering place among writers, painters, and poets in the early 1900s. It was the creative center of the city with jazz clubs and late-night discussion. Pablo Picasso and poet Guillaume Apollinaire met nightly in one café or another here, as did some well-known writers like Ernest Hemingway, Henry Miller, and Ezra Pound. After War World II, the area was never the same.

It was named for an adventurer who sowed a crop in Europe which is being harvested until today. I had often walked this street, sometimes with Hella, towards the river, often, without her, towards the girls of Montparnasse.

MONTPARNASSE TODAY

In 1972, Paris's tallest office building, the Montparnasse Tower was built and set a strikingly different tone for Montparnasse compared to the bohemian lifestyle that thrived in Baldwin's days. However, small café-theaters have sprung up in the past few years causing movie-goers to gravitate to the area and the most well-known cafés that once served the great writers and artists never left—the clientele has simply changed.

Not very long ago either, though it seemed, that morning, to have occurred in another life.

We were going to Les Halles for breakfast. We piled into a taxi, the four of us, unpleasantly crowded together, a circumstance which elicited from Jacques and Guillaume, a series of lewd speculations. The lewdness was particularly revolting in that it not only failed of wit, it was so clearly an expression of contempt and self-contempt; it bubbled upward out of them like a fountain of black water. It was clear that they were tantalizing themselves with Giovanni and me and this set my teeth on edge. But Giovanni leaned back against the taxi window, allowing his arm to press my shoulder lightly, seeming to say that we should soon be rid of these old men and should not be distressed that their dirty water splashed—we would have no trouble washing it away.

"Look," said Giovanni, as we crossed the river. "This old whore, Paris, as she turns in bed, is very moving."

I looked out, beyond his heavy profile, which was grey—from fatigue and from the light of the sky above us. The river was swollen and yellow. Nothing moved on the river. Barges were tied up along the banks. The island of the city widened away from us, bearing the weight of the cathedral; beyond this, dimly, through speed and mist, one made out the individual roofs of Paris, their myriad, squat chimney stacks very beautiful and varicolored under the pearly sky. Mist clung to the river, softening that army of trees, softening those stones, hiding the city's dreadful corkscrew alleys and dead-end streets, clinging like a curse to the men who slept beneath us, very black and lone, walking along the river.

"Some rats have gone in," said Giovanni, "and now other rats come out." He smiled bleakly and looked at me; to my surprise, he took my hand and held it. "Have you ever slept under a bridge?" he asked. "Or perhaps they have soft beds with warm blankets under the bridges in your country?"

I did not know what to do about my hand; it seemed better to do nothing. "Not yet," I said, "but I may. My hotel wants to throw me out."

I had said it lightly, with a smile, out of a desire to put myself, in terms of an acquaintance with wintry things, on an equal footing with him. But the fact that I had said it as he held my hand made it sound to me unutterably helpless and soft and coy. But I could not say anything to counteract this impression: to say anything more would confirm it. I pulled my hand away, pretending that I had done so in order to search for a cigarette.

Jacques lit it for me.

"Where do you live?" he asked Giovanni.

"Oh," said Giovanni "out. Far out. It is almost not Paris."

"He lives in a dreadful street, near *Nation*," said Guillaume, "among all the dreadful bourgeoisie and their piglike children."

"You failed to catch the children at the right age," said Jacques. "They go through a period, all too brief, *bélas!* when a pig is perhaps the *only* animal they do not call to mind." And, again to Giovanni: "In a hotel?"

"No," said Giovanni, and for the first time he seemed slightly uncomfortable. "I live in a maid's room."

"With a maid?"

"No," said Giovanni, and smiled, "the maid is I don't know where. You could certainly tell that there was no maid if you ever saw my room."

"I would love to," said Jacques.

"Then we will give a party for you one day," said Giovanni.

This, too courteous and too bald to permit any further questioning, nearly forced, nevertheless, a question from my lips. Guillaume looked briefly at Giovanni, who did not look at him but out into the morning, whistling. I had been making resolutions for the last six hours and now I made another one: to have this whole thing "out" with Giovanni as soon as I got him alone at Les Halles. I was going to have to tell him that he had made a mistake but that we could still be friends. But I could not be certain, really, that it might not be I who was making a mistake, blindly misreading everything—and out of necessities, then, too shameful to be uttered. I was in a box for I could see that, no matter how I turned, the hours of confession was upon me and could scarcely be averted; unless, of course, I leaped out of the cab, which would be the most terrible confession of all.

Now the cabdriver asked us where we wanted to go, for we had arrived at the choked boulevards and impassable side streets of Les Halles.

LES HALLES IN THE 1950S

Les Halles during Baldwin's day has more in common with the Les Halles Émile Zola knew in the 1800s than one might think. Up to that time little had changed, but it wasn't long after Baldwin wrote *Giovanni's Room* that the Market was forced to the outskirts of the city and the Forum was built.

Leeks, onions, cabbages, oranges, apples, potatoes, cauliflowers, stood gleaming in mounds all over, on the sidewalks, in the streets before great metal sheds. The sheds were blocks long and within the sheds were piled more fruit, more vegetables, in some sheds, fish, in some sheds, cheese, in some whole animals, lately slaughtered. It scarcely seemed possible that all of this could ever be eaten. But in a few hours it would all be gone and trucks would be arriving from all corners of France—and making their way, to the great profit of a beehive of middlemen, across the city of Paris—to feed the roaring multitude. Who were roaring now, at once wounding and charming the ear, before and behind, and on either side of our taxi—our taxi driver, and Giovanni, too, roared back. The multitude of Paris seems to be dressed in blue every day but Sunday, when, for the most part, they put on an unbelievably festive black. Here they were now, in blue, disputing, every inch, our passage, with their wagons, handtrucks, camions, their bursting baskets carried at an angle steeply self-confident on the back. A red-faced woman, burdened with fruit, shouted—to Giovanni, the driver, to the world—a particularly vivid *cochonnerie*, to which the driver and Giovanni, at once, at the top of their lungs, responded, though the fruit lady had already passed beyond our sight and perhaps no longer even remembered her precisely obscene conjectures. We crawled along, for no one had yet told the driver where to stop, and Giovanni and the driver, who had, it appeared, immediately upon entering Les Halles, been transformed into brothers, exchanged speculations, unflattering in the extreme, concerning the hygiene, language, private parts, and habits, of the citizens of Paris. (Jacques and Guillaume were exchanging speculations, unspeakably less good-natured, concerning every passing male.) The pavements were slick with leavings, mainly cast-off, rotten leaves, flowers, fruit, and vegetables which had met with disaster natural and slow, or abrupt. And the walls and corners were combed with *pissoirs*, dull-burning, make-shift braziers, cafes, restaurants, and smoky yellow bistros—of these last, some so small that they were little more than diamond-shaped, enclosed corners holding bottles and a zinc-covered counter. At all these points, men, young, old, middle-aged, powerful, powerful even in the various fashions in which they had met, or were meeting, their various ruin; and women, more than making up in shrewdness and patience, in an ability to count and weigh—and shout—whatever they might lack in muscle; though they did not, really, seem to lack much. Nothing here reminded me of home, though Giovanni recognized, revelled in it all.

School Girls, 1906

Claudine in Paris

BY COLETTE (1900)

Born Sidonie-Gabrielle Colette in the Burgundian village of Saint-Sauveur-en-Puisaye in 1873, Colette moved to Paris when she was twenty years old, and soon married writer and music critic Henri Gauthier-Villars (Monsieur Willy). The Claudine series of novels was originally published under her husband's name, since the idea of women writing was frowned upon at that time. Tired of Henri's affairs, Colette left him and explored her own sexuality by having relationships with both men and women. Her lack of inhibitions made her as famous as her writing—perhaps even more. In 1912, she married Henri de Jouvenel. This marriage lasted until 1924. Eleven years later she married Maurice Goudeket and changed her legal name to simply Sidonie Goudeket. Colette lived most of her life in one Paris apartment at 9 Rue de Beaujolais with a view of the Palais-Royal. She died in Paris in 1954.

Considered one of France's leading twentieth-century novelists, she created a sense of place in her subjective style, with a child-like sense of the world, an epicurean philosophy of life, and a musicality in her prose.

Claudine in Paris is the second of four installations in the Claudine series that Colette published under her first husband's pen name, Willy. Her creation of a rebellious young French woman—experiencing life, Paris, and marriage—made the series a huge success. In this section, Claudine, a teenager who has always lived her life in Montigny, France, learns that she and her father will be moving to Paris.

The following excerpt was translated from the original French text by Marie Emmanuelle Hartness.

FROM CHAPTER TWO

The journey, the arrival, the beginning of settling in are getting lost in a fog of anxiety. The dark apartment, between two courtyards on sordid, destitute rue Jacob, left me in a sorrowful stupor. Without moving, I saw the cases of books arrive one by one, and then the furniture in its new scenery; I watched Papa, excited and restless, hammering on shelves, pushing his desk from one corner to another, rejoicing at the location of the apartment: "just around the corner from La Sorbonne, very close to the Geographical Society, and library Sainte-Geneviève a hop, skip and jump away!"

THE SORBONNE

The name *Sorbonne* refers to the historic University of Paris founded in 1257 by Robert de Sorbon. The Collège de *Sorbonne*, as it was often called, was closed during the Revolution, but Napoléon reopened the institution in 1808. It finally closed in 1882, but the name *Sorbonne* lived on as the buildings were used for the Academy of Paris. In 1970, the University of Paris was divided into thirteen autonomous universities, but are managed under a common chancellor. Despite this reorganization, there is no system that binds the universities academically.

I heard Mélie whining about the smallness of her kitchen, despite it being on the other side of the landing, and in addition to it being one of the most beautiful rooms in the apartment; and I suffered after she served us, under the pretext of our unfinished and difficult settling-in, some foodstuff . . . which was unfinished and difficult to ingest. I was inhabited by only one thought: "How is it that *I myself* stand here, is it *me* who made this folly possible?" I refused to go out. I obstinately refused to take charge of anything useful; I wandered from one room to another, my throat constricted and I had no appetite whatsoever. After ten days I looked so queer that Papa himself noticed, panicking right away, because he does everything fully and without moderation. He put me on his knee, against his tricolor beard, and rocked me, holding me in his gnarled hands that smelled of pine from having built so many shelves . . . I said nothing while I gritted my teeth, because I was still harboring a fierce grudge against him . . . And then, my tense nerves finally gave in to an hysterical tantrum, and Mélie put me to bed, quite feverish.

* * *

My first outing took place in March. A sharp sun and an acid wind; Papa and myself in a carriage with inflatable tires. With my red cape from Montigny and my astrakhan polo, I look like a poor little boy in a skirt. (And my shoes having become so unwieldy!) Slow-paced strolls in the Luxembourg gardens, where my dear father entertained me with a comparison of the merits of the Nationale and the Sainte-Geneviève Libraries.

SAINTE-GENEVIÈVE LIBRARIES

In 1837 this already popular library added evening hours to accommodate its patrons (though women were not allowed to attend in the evenings until 1898). With these additional hours the number of visitors rose exponentially. In 1851 a new library was built and even still, patrons had to wait for a seat. During Colette's time the library continued growing in popularity. For example, in 1910, over 222,000 readers were admitted, compared to a combined total of 37,000 patrons visiting the other two libraries. Today it is an inter-university library for all thirteen campuses of the University of Paris.

The wind makes me dizzy, as does the sun. I find the long, broad planted rows quite beautiful, but the abundance of children and the absence of weeds shock me, one just as much as the other.

"While proofreading my great *Treatise*," Papa tells me, "I noticed that there is still a lot to dig up. The lack of depth of certain portions astonishes me. Don't you think it is strange, that, with my mental precision, I could only touch on certain important points—fascinating, if I may—specific to minute species? But these are not little girl stories."

Little girl! Will he not venture to remark that I am spreading my wings in a hurry, leaving seventeen years behind in the dust? And as for minute species, ah! la, la, what do I care! And the capitals, etcetera!

So many children, so many children! Will I, some day, have this many children? And who is the gentleman who shall so inspire me to perpetrate them with him? Tisk, tisk! It is strange, ever since I have been sick, my imagination and my nerves have become chaste. What would people think of a *Great Treatise?—my treatise*—about the moralizing influence of cerebral fever on young girls?

My poor little Luce . . . The trees bloom so early here! Lilacs are shooting out tender leaves. Back home, back home . . . we would only see brown, varnished buds, and at the most wild forest anemones, if that!

FROM CHAPTER FIVE

Well, let me tell you, it is not so terrible to go out by oneself in Paris. I brought back some very interesting observations from my little walk: 1. it is much, much warmer than in Montigny; 2. the inside of your nose is black when you get home; 3. people stare at you if you stand by yourself in front of the newspaper kiosk; 4. people also stare at you if you don't accept being treated with disrespect on the sidewalk.

Why don't I narrate the incident concerning observation number 4. A nice looking man was following me, rue des Saints-Pères.

During the first quarter-hour, internal jubilation for Claudine. Followed by a nice-looking man, like in Albert Guillaume's illustrations! The second quarter-hour: the man's steps come closer and I quicken mine, but he keeps his distance. Third quarter-hour: the man passes me, gooses my behind with a detached aloofness. Claudine leaps up with her umbrella and rains blows on the man's head, with all that good old Fresnois vigor. Man's hat in the gutter, immense delight of the passers-by, and disappearance of Claudine, overwhelmed by her unexpected success.

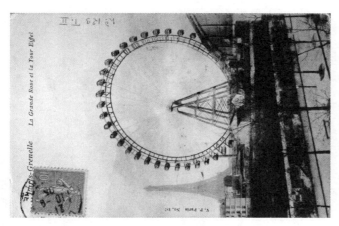

Ferris Wheel and Eiffel Tower, 1905

Capturing Paris

BY KATHARINE DAVIS (2006)

Born in 1948 in Summit, New Jersey, Katharine Davis moved to Switzerland as a young girl when her father's job transferred him to an office in Zurich. She attended boarding school and studied French three hours a day while studying American subjects only a few times a week. She returned to America to attend college at

Pine Manor in Wheaton, Massachusetts, where she studied French Literature. During this time her parents moved to Paris and she visited them frequently and got to know the city well. She went on to teach French for many years and only began to write her first novel, *Capturing Paris*, when she was fifty. Eight years later the novel was published.

Davis lives in Alexandria, Virginia, during the winters and York Harbor, Maine, during the summers. She credits her writing to years of reading great works both French and American, although mostly French.

Davis's style is carefully crafted and her characters are conflicted, which makes for a good story. Her ability to pace the novel appropriately is one of her greatest strengths. In *Capturing Paris*, Annie and Wesley Reed, an American couple have what appears to be a lovely existence in the Marais district of Paris, yet they find their marriage crumbling beneath them when he loses his job and she, a poet in the Liberal Arts Abroad Program, finally lands a job writing poetry to accompany photographs of Paris. As her career moves forward, and his slips away from him, their marriage becomes more troubled.

CHAPTER ONE

Annie Reed walked along the rue de Rennes wondering if her husband still loved her.

Paris was colder than usual that fall. She loved this time of day, *la crépuscule*, the nebulous period that floats between day and night. Her heels clicked as they struck the cold pavement. She wished that she had gone to the basement storage in her apartment building to take out her boots. The approach of winter had crept up on her. Gone were the golden dry October days, like those you saw in movies, where couples strolled along the Seine, pausing to look at old prints and books in open carts. The damp November air had already settled into her bones.

THE RUE DE RENNES

This street, which spans between Boulevard St. Germain and Boulevard Montparnasse, is a must for those who want to add a bit of the Parisian style to their wardrobe. On the St. Germain end are the higher-priced restaurants and boutiques, though a cafeteria and a grocery store are still there. Toward the Montparnasse end is a large bookstore, and theater performances, but clothing boutiques and souvenir shops line the street from one end to the other. There's also the outdoor organic farmer's market twice a week at Boulevard Raspail that should not be missed.

Dreary, dark, dusk—words she was trying to put into a poem on the seasonal shifts that changed the mood and tempo of the city. She admired the French poets who were able to capture the feel of the tight cold air, the closing down and pulling in particular to this time of year. The French language had a musical quality, a natural lyricism, that belied the darker message within. Annie wanted to capture this feeling in English. She wished she could breathe in the poignant beauty and exhale the words and images onto the page. She could hear the words, like puzzle pieces floating in her head, but she struggled to find the flow, the thread that would order the images and bring them to life.

Why did she bother? She tried not to think of the envelope in her briefcase. Stopped at a red light, she drew her shoulders up and released them, trying to get rid of the tension in her neck.

Her job at the Liberal Arts Abroad program had kept her cooped up in an overheated office all afternoon. She had published only a few poems in the last few years. She wanted her poetry to take precedence again, not easy after years of being busy with other things. Wesley certainly didn't seem to care. A thick sheet of ice had formed between them.

Annie arrived at the subway station and descended toward the rumbling trains. She pushed open the steel-and-glass door at the bottom of the steps, trying not to inhale the warm, dirty air rising from the tunnels below. Annie disliked crowds and walked toward the far end of the platform hoping to find a less busy spot to wait. She longed to be home; being with people all day tired her. The dark tunnels hummed with the possibility of approaching trains.

On the opposite platform Annie noticed an unusually tall young woman in a brilliant blue cape. She had to be foreign. When Annie moved to Paris over twenty years ago with Wesley and baby daughter Sophie in tow, she'd wanted to fit in, to look French. She loved the way French women dressed; understated, discreetly fashionable, they wore their clothes confidently, hinting at sexiness, suggesting the unexpected. Most of the women here on the subway platforms wore coats in subtle colors—brown, gray, or black—with perhaps a bright scarf arranged artfully at the neck. The first thing Annie had noticed when she moved from New York was the French addiction to scarves.

The woman across the platform looked like an exotic bird, unafraid to flaunt its colorful plumage. The theatrical-looking cape had a black velvet collar and could have been from a vintage clothing shop had it been more worn and faded. Her honey-colored hair fell heavily, just reaching her broad shoulders. She was more handsome than beautiful, with wide-set eyes and a full mouth.

Annie though of Baudelaire's words, "Luxe, calme, et volupte." She knew she shouldn't stare, but her eyes kept going back to the woman. There was something disconnected about her. She looked calm, almost dreamy. While probably in her thirties, the age of a young mother, she didn't have the intense, fixed look of a mother eager to get to the school, or day care center to find her children.

Moments later a train pulled up to the opposite platform, stirring up the odor of wet clothing, tired bodies, and stale air. Passengers jostled their way into the full cars, and Annie lost sight of the woman. The train pulled out of the station and she experienced a momentary feeling of loss when she looked back at the empty place where the woman had stood. Why had this woman caught her attention? Lately she found herself contemplating other women's lives. Studying the faces around her, particularly women close to her own age, Annie wondered if they too felt the ache of an empty nest, or faced unhappy husbands at the end of the day. Her own train arrived and screeched to a halt. The doors slid open. Annie clutched her briefcase and got ready to board the crowded car.

Darkness blanketed the city when Annie emerged at her Metro stop, Hôtel de Ville, in the Fourth Arrondissement.

ARRONDISSEMENTS

Paris is divided into twenty arrondissements, identified through the last two numbers in Parisian postal codes. The Fourth Arrondissement is centrally located in the city and home to some of the more medieval sites of Paris; most famous is the Notre Dame Cathedral. With the addition of the George Pompidou Center in 1977, the fourth has even more to offer now as the Center houses some of the best in contemporary art.

City of Lights, she thought, what a misnomer in November. A cold mist, not quite a drizzle, gave the streets an oily sheen. Drivers blew their horns impatiently in the heavy traffic. Annie looked at the closed shutters of the apartments above the street. She loved the sight of lamplight seeping out between the louvers. At the end of the afternoon, she relished going from room to room in her own apartment closing the outside shutters and drawing the curtains. The sense of warmth and enclosure of a home tucked in for the evening filled her with pleasure.

She used to love coming home and having an hour or two alone when she would putter, look at the mail that the concierge had slipped under the door, and start to put dinner together. She might take out her poems and revise work that she had started that morning. Late afternoon, with its dense quiet, was a productive time of day for her. Now Wesley would be there, awaiting her return.

Rue de Seine, 1908

892. PARIS — Rue de Seine

A Tale of Two Cities

BY CHARLES DICKENS (1859)

Born February 7, 1812, in Portsmouth, Hampshire, England, Charles Dickens was the second child of eight and began his life in a large home with two live-in servants. Charles's father, John Dickens, a clerk in the Navy Pay Office, was a kind man, but a man who seemed unable to live within his means. In 1824, John

Dickens was forced into the Marshalsea debtor's prison. This dramatically changed the family's way of life and Charles's mother insisted that he help support the family by working at a shoe blacking factory. He was twelve. By the time he was a teenager, Dickens had lived in two very different worlds—that of the well-to-do and that of the working poor. His father did manage to send Charles to Wellington House Academy in London in 1825, but was unable to sustain the cost of such an education so Charles had to leave and take a job clerking for a law firm.

In 1836, Charles became editor for *Bentley's Miscellany*, in which *Pickwick Papers* was first serialized. That same year, he married Catherine Hogarth. They lived in London and would have ten children together.

Dickens left *Bentley's* in 1839 and moved his family to Regent's Park. In 1842, he visited the United States and Canada (he was extremely popular in the States) and in 1844 he went to Italy and Switzerland. All the while, Dickens wrote and people waited with great anticipation for the next installment of his work. In 1865, while returning to London from Paris, Dickens was in a brutal train crash. Though he escaped the wreck practically unharmed, Dickens was never the same. Most noticeable was the degree to which his writing slowed. He died in 1870 at his home, Gad's Hill, and is buried in the Poet's Corner of Westminster Abbey, London.

While Dickens aimed to please his readers, he maintained his conviction to write about social injustice. He wanted the rich to know how the poor lived and the poor to understand how the rich spent their time. Most of Dickens's novels were written in monthly or weekly installments. He paid attention to his readers' reactions to one chapter before completing or sometimes even beginning the next. He had the rare ability to write these episodic installments with masterful cliff-hangers and still create a coherent novel in the end. His gifts for writing poetically and satirically and for creating unforgettable characters (with unforgettable names) are reasons why Dickens's novels have never gone out of print.

A Tale of Two Cities was written in thirty-one weekly installments beginning in April of 1859. The story is set in a tranquil London and a turbulent Paris before and during the French Revolution. Unlike most of his novels there is far less comic relief, and the story is not as character-driven as his other works. There is Charles Darnay, the French aristocrat who falls victim to the revolution, and Sydney Carton, an Englishman who loves Darnay's wife, but as seen in the two sections selected, the storyline is driven by the events that unfold in Paris more than the characters.

FROM BOOK ONE, CHAPTER FIVE, "THE WINE-SHOP"

The wine was red wine, and had stained the ground of the narrow street in the suburb of Saint Antoine, in Paris, where it was spilled. It had stained many hands, too, and many faces, and many naked feet, and many wooden shoes. The hands of the man who sawed the wood, left red marks on the billets; and the forehead of the woman who nursed her baby, was stained with the stain of the old rag she wound about her head again. Those who had been greedy with the staves of the cask, had acquired a tigerish smear about the mouth; and one tall joker so besmirched, his head more out of a long squalid bag of a nightcap than in it, scrawled upon a wall with his finger dipped in muddy wine-lees—BLOOD.

The time was to come, when that wine too would be spilled on the street-stones, and when the stain of it would be red upon many there.

And now that the cloud settled on Saint Antoine, which a momentary gleam had driven from his sacred countenance, the darkness of it was heavy—cold, dirt, sickness, ignorance, and want, were the lords in waiting on the saintly presence—nobles of great power all of them; but, most especially the last. Samples of a people that had undergone a terrible grinding and regrinding in the mill, and certainly not in the fabulous mill which ground old people young, shivered at every corner, passed in and out at every doorway, looked from every window, fluttered in every vestige of a garment that the wind shook. The mill which had worked them down, was the mill that grinds young people old; the children had ancient faces and grave voices; and upon them, and upon the grown faces, and ploughed into every furrow of age and coming up afresh, was the sign, Hunger. It was prevalent everywhere. Hunger was pushed out of the tall houses, in the wretched clothing that hung upon poles and lines; Hunger was patched into them with straw and rag and wood and paper; Hunger was repeated in every fragment of the small modicum of firewood that the man sawed off; Hunger stared down from the smokeless chimneys, and started up from the filthy street that had no offal, among its refuse, of anything to eat. Hunger was the inscription on the baker's shelves, written in every small loaf of his scanty stock of bad bread; at the sausage-shop, in every dead-dog preparation that was offered for sale. Hunger rattled its dry bones among the roasting chestnuts in the turned cylinder; Hunger was shred into atomics in every far-thing porringer of husky chips of potato, fried with some reluctant drops of oil.

Its abiding place was in all things fitted to it. A narrow winding street, full of offence and stench, with other narrow winding streets diverging, all peopled by rags and nightcaps, and all smelling of rags and nightcaps, and all visible things with a brooding look upon them that looked ill. In the hunted air of the people there was yet some wild-beast thought of the possibility of turning at bay. Depressed and slinking though they were, eyes of fire were not wanting among them; nor compressed lips, white with what they suppressed; nor foreheads knitted into the likeness of the gallows-rope they mused about enduring, or inflicting. The trade signs (and they were almost as many as the shops) were, all, grim illustrations of Want. The butcher and the porkman painted up, only the leanest scrags of meat; the baker, the coarsest of meagre loaves. The people rudely pictured as drinking in the wine-shops, croaked over their scanty measures of thin wine and beer, and were gloweringly confidential together.

Nothing was represented in a flourishing condition, save tools and weapons; but, the cutler's knives and axes were sharp and bright, the smith's hammers were heavy, and the gunmaker's stock was murderous.

The crippling stones of the pavement, with their many little reservoirs of mud and water, had no footways, but broke off abruptly at the doors. The kennel, to make amends, ran down the middle of the street—when it ran at all: which was only after heavy rains, and then it ran, by many eccentric fits, into the houses. Across the streets, at wide intervals, one clumsy lamp was slung by a rope and pulley; at night, when the lamplighter had let these down, and lighted, and hoisted them again, a feeble grove of dim wicks swung in a sickly manner overhead, as if they were at sea. Indeed they were at sea, and the ship and crew were in peril of tempest.

For, the time was to come, when the gaunt scarecrows of that region should have watched the lamplighter, in their idleness and hunger, so long, as to conceive the idea of improving on his method, and hauling up men by those ropes and pulleys, to flare upon the darkness of their condition. But, the time was not come yet; and every wind that blew over France shook the rags of the scarecrows in vain, for the birds, fine of song and feather, took no warning.

FROM BOOK TWO, CHAPTER SEVEN, "MONSEIGNEUR IN TOWN"

Monseigneur, one of the great lords in power at the Court, held his fortnightly reception in his grand hotel in Paris. Monseigneur was in his inner room, his sanctuary of sanctuaries, the Holiest of Holiest to the crowd of worshippers in the suite of rooms without. Monseigneur was about to take his chocolate. Monseigneur could swallow a great many things with ease, and was by some few sullen minds supposed to be rather rapidly swallowing France; but, his morning's chocolate could not so much as get into the throat of Monseigneur, without the aid of four strong men besides the Cook.

CHOCOLATE

When first introduced to chocolate, the French court was skeptical of it. They only accepted it after the Paris faculty of medicine approved it. The dessert, which was very expensive and only sold in the form of cocoa or liquid until 1879, became the drink of the French court under Louis XIII.

Yes. It took four men, all four ablaze with gorgeous decoration, and the Chief of them unable to exist with fewer than two gold watches in his pocket, emulative of the noble and chaste fashion set by Monseigneur, to conduct the happy chocolate to Monseigneur's lips. One lacquey carried the chocolate-pot into the sacred presence; a second, milled and frothed the chocolate with the little instrument he bore for that function; a third, presented the favoured napkin; a fourth (he of the two gold watches), poured the chocolate out. It was impossible for Monseigneur to dispense with one of these attendants on the chocolate and hold his high place under the admiring Heavens. Deep would have been the blot upon his escutcheon if his chocolate had been ignobly waited on by only three men; he must have died of two.

Monseigneur had been out at a little supper last night, where the Comedy and the Grand Opera were charmingly represented. Monseigneur was out at a little supper most nights, with fascinating company.

GRAND OPERA

Grand Opera is most often associated with productions of the Paris Opera from the 1820s to the 1850s. In general terms, however, it is a genre of nineteenth-century opera with lavish stage designs, large casts and orchestras, and plots that center around historic events. As the Grand Opera progressed in Paris it came to include extravagant ballet performances.

So polite and so impressible was Monseigneur, that the Comedy and the Grand Opera had far more influence with him in the tiresome articles of state affairs and state secrets, than the needs of all

France. A happy circumstance for France, as the like always is for all countries similarly favoured!—always was for England (by way of example), in the regretted days of the merry Stuart who sold it.

Monseigneur had one truly noble idea of general public business, which was, to let everything go on in its own way; of particular public business, Monseigneur had the other truly noble idea that it must all go his way—tend to his own power and pocket. Of his pleasures, general and particular, Monseigneur had the other truly noble idea, that the world was made for them. The text of his order (altered from the original by only a pronoun, which is not much) ran: "The earth and the fulness thereof are mine, saith Monseigneur."

Yet, Monseigneur had slowly found that vulgar embarrassments crept into his affairs, both private and public; and he had, as to both classes of affairs, allied himself perforce with a Farmer-General. As to finances public, because Monseigneur could not make anything at all of them, and must consequently let them out to somebody who could; as to finances private, because Farmer-Generals were rich, and Monseigneur, after generations of great luxury and expense, was growing poor. Hence Monseigneur had taken his sister from a convent, while there was yet time to ward off the impending veil, the cheapest garment she could wear, and had bestowed her as a prize upon a very rich Farmer-General, poor in family. Which Farmer-General, carrying an appropriate cane with a golden apple on the top of it, was now among the company in the outer rooms, much prostrated before by mankind—always excepting superior mankind of the blood of Monseigneur, who, his own wife included, looked down upon him with the loftiest contempt.

A sumptuous man was the Farmer-General. Thirty horses stood in his stables, twenty-four male domestics sat in his halls, six body-women waited on his wife. As one who pretended to do nothing but plunder and forage where he could, the Farmer-General—howsoever his matrimonial relations conduced to social morality—was at least the greatest reality among the personages who attended at the hotel of Monseigneur that day.

For, the rooms, though a beautiful scene to look at, and adorned with every device of decoration that the taste and skill of the time could achieve, were, in truth, not a sound business; considered with any reference to the scarecrows in the rags and nightcaps elsewhere (and not so far off, either, but that the watching towers of Notre Dame, almost equidistant from the two extremes, could see them both), they would have been an exceedingly uncomfortable business—if that could have been anybody's business, at the house of Monseigneur.

Military officers destitute of military knowledge; naval officers with no idea of a ship; civil officers without a notion of affairs; brazen ecclesiastics, of the worst world worldly, with sensual eyes, loose tongues, and looser lives; all totally unfit for their several callings, all lying horribly in pretending to belong to them, but all nearly or remotely of the order of Monseigneur, and therefore foisted on all public employments from which anything was to be got; these were to be told off by the score and the score. People not immediately connected with Monseigneur or the State, yet equally unconnected with anything that was real, or with lives passed in travelling by any straight road to any true earthly end, were no less abundant. Doctors who made great fortunes out of dainty remedies for imaginary disorders that never existed, smiled upon their courtly patients in the ante-chambers of Monseigneur. Projectors who had discovered every kind of remedy for the little evils with which the State was touched, except the remedy of setting to work in earnest to root out a single sin, poured their distracting babble into any ears they could lay hold of, at the reception of Monseigneur. Unbelieving Philosophers who were remodelling the world with words, and making card-towers of Babel to scale the skies with, talked with Unbelieving Chemists who had an eye on the transmutation of metals, at this wonderful gathering accumulated by Monseigneur. Exquisite gentlemen of the finest breeding, which was at that remarkable time—and has been since—to be known by its fruits of indifference to every natural subject of human interest, were in the most exemplary state of exhaustion, at the hotel of Monseigneur. Such homes had these various notabilities left behind them in the fine world of Paris, that the spies among the assembled devotees of Monseigneur—forming a goodly half of the polite company—would have found it hard to discover among the angels of that sphere one solitary wife, who, in her manners and appearance, owned to being a Mother. Indeed, except for the mere act of bringing a troublesome creature into this world—which does not go far towards the realisation of the name of mother—there was no such thing known to the fashion. Peasant women kept the unfashionable babies close, and brought them up, and charming grandmammas of sixty dressed and supped as at twenty.

The leprosy of unreality disfigured every human creature in attendance upon Monseigneur. In the outermost room were half a dozen exceptional people who had had, for a few years, some vague misgiving in them that things in general were going rather wrong. As a promising way of setting them right, half of the half-dozen had become members of a fantastic sect of Convulsionists, and were even then considering within themselves whether they should foam, rage, roar, and turn cataleptic on the spot—thereby setting up a highly intelligible finger-post to the Future, for Monseigneur's guidance. Besides these Dervishes, were other three who had rushed into another sect, which mended matters with a jargon about "the Centre of Truth": holding that Man had got out of the Centre of Truth—which did not need much demonstration—but had not got out of the Circumference, and that he was to be kept from flying out of the Circumference, and was even to be shoved back into the Centre, by fasting and seeing of spirits. Among these, accordingly, much discoursing with spirits went on—and it did a world of good which never became manifest.

But, the comfort was, that all the company at the grand hotel of Monseigneur were perfectly dressed. If the Day of Judgment had only been ascertained to be a dress day, everybody there would have been eternally correct. Such frizzling and powdering and sticking up of hair, such delicate complexions artificially preserved and mended, such gallant swords to look at, and such delicate honour to the sense of smell, would surely keep anything going, for ever and ever.

The exquisite gentlemen of the finest breeding wore little pendent trinkets that chinked as they languidly moved; these golden fetters rang like precious little bells; and what with that ringing, and with the rustle of silk and brocade and fine linen, there was a flutter in the air that fanned Saint Antoine and his devouring hunger far away.

Dress was the one unfailing talisman and charm used for keeping all things in their places. Everybody was dressed for a Fancy Ball that was never to leave off. From the Palace of the Tuileries, through Monseigneur and the whole Court, through the Chambers, the Tribunals of Justice, and all society (except the scarecrows), the Fancy Ball descended to the Common Executioner:

who, in pursuance of the charm, was required to officiate "frizzled, powdered, in a gold-laced coat, pumps, and white silk stockings."

THE PALAIS DE TUILERIES AND THE GARDEN

The Palace was originally built in 1564 for the widow of Henry II of France. It served as Louis XIV's home while Versailles was built, but once the French Revolution began he was forced to return to the Tuileries under house arrest. He tried to escape in June of 1791 but was captured and sent back. The palace was later invaded by a mob forcing the royal family to flee through the garden and take refuge with the Legislative Assembly. After the Palais de Tuileries was demolished in 1882, the Tuileries Gardens were all that remained.

At the gallows and the wheel—the axe was a rarity—Monsieur Paris, as it was the episcopal mode among his brother Professors of the provinces, Monsieur Orleans, and the rest, to call him, presided in this dainty dress. And who among the company at Monseigneur's reception in that seventeen hundred and eightieth year of our Lord, could possibly doubt, that a system rooted in a frizzled hangman, powdered, gold-laced, pumped, and white-silk stockinged, would see the very stars out!

Monseigneur having eased his four men of their burdens and taken his chocolate, caused the doors of the Holiest of Holiests to be thrown open, and issued forth. Then, what submission, what cringing and fawning, what servility, what abject humiliation! As to bowing down in body and spirit, nothing in that way was left for Heaven—which may have been one among other reasons why the worshippers of Monseigneur never troubled it.

PARIS. — La Gare de Lyon

73

Gare de Lyon, 1908

As They Were

BY M. F. K. FISHER (1983)

Mary Frances Kennedy was born in Michigan in 1908 to Episcopalian parents in a Quaker community. In 1910, the family moved to Whittier, California. She attended the University of California and while there, in 1929, she met and married Alfred Fisher. They spent the first three years of their marriage in Europe, mostly in Dijon—the gastronomical capital of France where she enjoyed studying at the University of Dijon. In 1932, they moved back to southern California and she taught at Occidental College. Fisher

No 33

left her husband, Alfred, for a man that she referred to in her books as "Chexbres." Their marriage, though passionate, ended quickly and tragically after he killed himself in 1941. In 1992, M. F. K. Fisher died in her home in California from Parkinson's disease at the age of eighty-three.

Inspired by an Elizabethan cookbook she read while at the Los Angeles Public Library, Fisher began writing essays about her cooking experiences. Her first book, *Serve It Forth*, published in 1937, was thought to have been written by a man because it didn't read the way women typically wrote about cooking. Over time, the way she wrote about food became accepted and respected. Her prose, undeniably skillful and elegant, drew respect and readers far beyond the world of cooking. She is known as one of the best food writers in both America and France.

In all of her twenty books food was her primary theme, as she saw it as one of the "arts of life." The art of living well and appreciating the beauty of life was a secondary theme in her essays.

As They Were is a collection of essays about Fisher's travels throughout the world and her love of French food and appreciation for life. As always, her writing style is direct, sophisticated, and centered around the fine art of eating and living well. It's a delightful compilation of essays for anyone traveling through France with a hearty appetite.

In the essay titled "Gare de Lyon," Fisher recalls the day she and her father experienced the newly constructed railway terminal.

FROM "GARE DE LYON"

It was perhaps different in 1900. The hunger and shame of the Franco-Prussian War had been half forgotten by a new generation, and the Dreyfus Affair seemed temporarily under wraps. Paris needed and indeed deserved a circus. Architects were appointed, perhaps subconsciously, who could evoke all the rich weightiness of the Third Empire, before the late and current troubles, and they put together some pleasure domes for their fair that still enchant us: two palaces, the Grand and the Petit; the bridge across the Seine named for Alexander the Third; best of all to some at least, the Gare de Lyon.

PONT ALEXANDRE III

Built from 1896 to 1900, this bridge was quite an engineering accomplishment for its time with its high single steel arch. It was named in honor of Tsar Alexander III and styled with Art Nouveau lamps, cherubs, and winged horses in an effort to blend in with the opulent Grand Palais. Among the most interesting ornamental features of the bridge are the gilded statues, each honoring a different artist. The bridge is still considered the most extravagant if not the most beautiful bridge in the city.

It happened before my time, and the French accounts are understandably vague about how and when that World's Fair finally ground into action.

It seems natural, by now, that the enormous glassy station was formally inaugurated a year later, but it is still there to prove that in 1901, on April seventeenth, the President of the Republic and countless international notables gathered in it to declare that the Gare de Lyon was indeed a reality.

GARE DE LYON

Named after one of its most popular stops, Lyon, this is one of the six large railway stations in Paris. The station's French National Railway Company services run to the south and east of France. It was built for the World's Fair of 1900, and has a beautiful ornately decorated restaurant, where Fisher most likely ate on occasion, called the Le Train Bleu.

No doubt other very solemn things have happened there in almost a century, like treaty signings and top-level hanky-panky connected with both railroads and people, and municipal banquets, but it is hard to imagine that they did not contain a certain element of enjoyment, in that magical place. Surely the ceremonial toasts tasted better there . . .

As far as I can know or learn, no other railroad station in the world manages so mysteriously to cloak with compassion the anguish of departure and the dubious ecstasies of return and arrival. Any waiting room in the world is filled with all this, and I have sat in many of them and accepted it, and I know from deliberate acquaintance that the whole human experience is more bearable at the Gare de Lyon in Paris than anywhere else. By now the public rooms on the train level are more plastic-topped, chromium-benched, than in the first days of wood everywhere, with iron and brass fittings. But the porters seem to stay sturdy and aware, and there is a near-obsolete courtesy at the "snack bars," even five minutes before commute time.

For me, it began to come to life in 1937. I was there often, from 1929 on, always one more ant scuttling for a certain track, a cheap train south to Dijon, a luxury train to Lausanne. The station was something to run through. It was a grimy glass tunnel, and I felt glad when we pulled out and headed south.

But in 1937, when I could meet my parents in La Ville Lumière, I grew almost shockingly aware of the station. I went there early that twilight, to wait for their train.

LA VILLE LUMIÈRE

Paris's most well-known nickname is La Ville Lumière, which translated into English is "City of Light." The name was given for the city's early and dedicated use of street lights as well as its welcoming atmosphere for new ideas.

On the quai that looked far out under the glass roof and along all the gleaming tracks was a café, part of the big noisy brasserie inside. There were little trees in long boxes, to sweeten the air and catch the soot, and the tables were of that grey-white marble that apparently was created by Nature solely for café tabletops. I sat waiting, drinking a brandy and water, realizing suddenly that I was not in a station, but in a place.

My family arrived, worn after a rough crossing, and it was not for perhaps ten days that I went back. My father was going down to Nice. For the first of countless times I cunningly arranged our getting around Paris so that we would have to wait for the train to slide in under the glass roof along the silver track, so that I could be there . . . in the place.

It was one of the pleasantest times I'd ever known with a man I'd always respected and loved. We were two people, suddenly. We sat behind the boxes filled with gritty treelings, and although it was only late morning we drank slowly at brandy again, with water and casual talk and mostly a quiet awareness of the loveliness of the great station.

It was not noisy. It was not stuffy. People did not look sad or even hurried. Trains whistled and chugged in and out, slid voluptuously toward us and then stopped. Big boards lit up here and there, high above the tracks, telling people where to go, when. A porter came to tell me that it was time for the gentleman to board.

"This is the way to do it! How can a railroad station be so beautiful?" my father asked happily, and I knew that I had marked off another mile in my life.

PARIS - Palais du Luxembourg.

Palais du Luxembourg, 1908

Madame Bovary

BY GUSTAVE FLAUBERT (1856)

Born in 1821 in Rouen, France, Gustave Flaubert attempted to study law until he was struck with a nervous disease thought to have been epilepsy. "I was cowardly in my youth," he wrote to his friend George Sand. "I was afraid of life." The disease changed him and from that point on, he lived exactly as he saw fit. He quit law school and began writing and studying literature.

His father, supportive of his decision, bought him a house in Croisset, on the Seine River, so he could have a quiet place to write. Upon his father's death however, Flaubert returned to Rouen and lived with his mother.

It seems Flaubert only fell in love once, and when that relationship ended in heartache he resigned himself to his work and his friendships. Among his friends was writer Maxime du Camp whom he traveled with through Turkey, Egypt, Northern Africa, and Europe between the years 1849 and 1851. When he returned from his travels he also returned to his mother's home where he began writing *Madame Bovary*. Flaubert died of a cerebral hemorrhage on May 8, 1880.

In the 1870s critics and scholars began calling Flaubert a naturalistic writer. They viewed it as a compliment, but he did not appreciate having labels put on his work. The label that has proven unshakable is that of a realist. What is sometimes overlooked, and underappreciated, is his intense labor over the precise words, tone, and style to use in every line in order to tell his story.

Madame Bovary, Flaubert's most famous novel, took him five years to write and was published in a serialized fashion in the *Revue de Paris* in 1856. The French government charged both Flaubert and his publisher on the grounds of immorality, but both were acquitted. By the time the novel was published in book form, it was well received. Though it is the only work in this anthology that is not set in Paris, travelers may relate to Emma Bovary's dreams of one day going to Paris. Emma, a country doctor's wife who is immature, unfaithful, and lives beyond her means, fantasizes of living in Paris among nobility. She reads novels, travel books, and even studies maps in her efforts to escape the country life that bores her.

FROM PART ONE, CHAPTER NINE

Often when Charles was out she took from the cupboard, between the folds of the linen where she had left it, the green silk cigar case. She looked at it, opened it, and even smelt the odour of the lining—a mixture of verbena and tobacco. Whose was it? The Viscount's? Perhaps it was a present from his mistress. It had been embroidered on some rosewood frame, a pretty little thing, hidden from all eyes, that had occupied many hours, and over which had fallen the soft curls of the pensive worker. A breath of love had passed over the stitches on the canvas; each prick of the needle had fixed there a hope or a memory, and all those interwoven threads of silk were but the continuity of the same silent passion. And then one morning the Viscount had taken it away with him. Of what had they spoken when it lay upon the wide-mantelled chimneys between flower-vases and Pompadour clocks? She was at Tostes; he was at Paris now, far away! What was this Paris like? What a vague name! She repeated it in a low voice, for the mere pleasure of it; it rang in her ears like a great cathedral bell; it shone before her eyes, even on the labels of her pomade-pots.

At night, when the carriers passed under her windows in their carts singing the "Marjolaine," she awoke, and listened to the noise of the iron-bound wheels, which, as they gained the country road, was soon deadened by the soil. "They will be there to-morrow!" she said to herself.

And she followed them in thought up and down the hills, traversing villages, gliding along the highroads by the light of the stars. At the end of some indefinite distance there was always a confused spot, into which her dream died.

She bought a plan of Paris, and with the tip of her finger on the map she walked about the capital. She went up the boulevards, stopping at every turning, between the lines of the streets, in front of the white squares that represented the houses. At last she would close the lids of her weary eyes, and see in the darkness the gas jets flaring in the wind and the steps of carriages lowered with much noise before the peristyles of theatres.

She took in "La Corbeille," a lady's journal, and the "Sylphe des Salons." She devoured, without skipping a word, all the accounts of first nights, races, and soirees, took interest in the debut of a singer, in the opening of a new shop. She knew the latest fashions, the addresses of the best tailors, the days of the Bois and the Opera.

In Eugene Sue she studied descriptions of furniture; she read Balzac and George Sand, seeking in them imaginary satisfaction for her own desires. Even at table she had her book by her, and turned over the pages while Charles ate and talked to her. The memory of the Viscount always returned as she read. Between him and the imaginary personages she made comparisons. But the circle of which he was the centre gradually widened round him,

BOIS DE BOULOGNE

By *Bois*, Flaubert refers to the forest-like park just west of the city. Napoléon III made the area into a park in 1852. The transformation from forest to park was financed by selling building lots along the north end of the Bois. The beauty of the park inspired both Van Gogh and Monet. Today, it is still a popular place for Parisians to go for fishing, boating, and picnics. The park also has two horse racing tracks and tennis courts are on the edge of the grounds. After dark, however, it is a popular place for prostitution.

and the aureole that he bore, fading from his form, broadened out beyond, lighting up her other dreams.

Paris, more vague than the ocean, glimmered before Emma's eyes in an atmosphere of vermilion. The many lives that stirred amid this tumult were, however, divided into parts, classed as distinct pictures. Emma perceived only two or three that hid from her all the rest, and in themselves represented all humanity. The world of ambassadors moved over polished floors in drawing rooms lined with mirrors, round oval tables covered with velvet and gold-fringed cloths. There were dresses with trains, deep mysteries, anguish hidden beneath smiles. Then came the society of the duchesses; all were pale; all got up at four o'clock; the women, poor angels, wore English point on their petticoats; and the men, unappreciated geniuses under a frivolous outward seeming, rode horses to death at pleasure parties, spent the summer season at Baden, and towards the forties married heiresses. In the private rooms of restaurants, where one sups after midnight by the light of wax candles, laughed the motley crowd of men of letters and actresses. They were prodigal as kings, full of ideal, ambitious, fantastic frenzy. This was an existence outside that of all others, between heaven and earth, in the midst of storms, having something of the sublime. For the rest of the world it was lost, with no particular place and as if non-existent. The nearer things were, moreover, the more her thoughts turned away from them. All her immediate surroundings, the wearisome country, the middle-class imbeciles, the mediocrity of existence, seemed to her exceptional, a peculiar chance that had caught hold of her, while beyond stretched, as far as eye could see, an immense land of joys and passions. She confused in her desire the sensualities of luxury with the delights of the heart, elegance of manners with delicacy of sentiment. Did not love, like Indian plants, need a special soil, a particular temperature? Signs by moonlight, long embraces, tears flowing over yielded hands, all the fevers of the flesh and the languors of tenderness could not be separated from the balconies of great castles full of indolence, from boudoirs with silken curtains and thick carpets, well-filled flower-stands, a bed on a raised dais, nor from the flashing of precious stones and the shoulder-knots of liveries.

CAFÉ DE LA PAIX

Emma Bovary longed to go to the Opera, and if Flaubert had written his novel just a few years later, he would have surely mentioned Café de la Paix by name as it was established in the Grand Hotel in 1862 across the street from the Opéra de Paris Garnier. With the exception of closing its doors briefly in 1939 in order to restore its second empire grandeur, the café has been a constant in Parisian dining—meeting even the highest expectations.

The lad from the posting house who came to groom the mare every morning passed through the passage with his heavy wooden shoes; there were holes in his blouse; his feet were bare in list slippers. And this was the groom in knee-britches with whom she had to be content! His work done, he did not come back again all day, for Charles on his return put up his horse himself, unsaddled him and put on the halter, while the servant-girl brought a bundle of straw and threw it as best she could into the manger.

To replace Nastasie (who left Tostes shedding torrents of tears) Emma took into her service a young girl of fourteen, an orphan with a sweet face. She forbade her wearing cotton caps, taught her to address her in the third person, to bring a glass of water on a plate, to knock before coming into a room, to iron, starch, and to dress her—wanted to make a lady's-maid of her. The new servant obeyed without a murmur, so as not to be sent away; and as madame usually left the key in the sideboard, Felicite every evening took a small supply of sugar that she ate alone in her bed after she had said her prayers.

Sometimes in the afternoon she went to chat with the postilions. Madame was in her room upstairs. She wore an open dressing gown that showed between the shawl facings of her bodice a pleated chamisette with three gold buttons. Her belt was a corded girdle with great tassels, and her small garnet coloured slippers had a large knot of ribbon that fell over her instep. She had bought herself a blotting book, writing case, pen-holder, and envelopes, although she had no one to write to; she dusted her what-not, looked at herself in the glass, picked up a book, and then, dreaming between the lines, let it drop on her knees. She longed to travel or to go back to her convent. She wished at the same time to die and to live in Paris.

Boulevard Saint-Germain, 1910

I Wish Someone Were Waiting for Me Somewhere

BY ANNA GAVALDA (1999)

Born in 1970 in Boulogne-Billancourt, Hauts-de-Seine, an upper-class neighborhood on the outskirts of Paris, Anna Gavalda is considered one of the most talented new voices in French literature. Once a high school French teacher, she now lives with her two daughters in the small city of Melun, Seine-et-Marne, southeast of

Paris and writes her novels and short stories. She also contributes regularly to *Elle.*

Gavalda's work has been commended for its originality, and has become a common selection in schools worldwide in recent years. Her stories center around love and loneliness, thereby having an international appeal, but there is no mistaking the Parisian quality of her work. By writing with such honesty about the vulnerabilities of today's Parisian culture where a quarter of the population lives alone, she has managed to strike a chord. She published her first collection of short stories, *I Wish Someone Were Waiting for Me Somewhere*, in 1999. The book has since been translated into several languages. Since that time she has published two novels: *Someone I Loved* (2002) and *Hunting and Gathering* (2004).

This excerpt, "Courting Rituals of the Saint-Germain-des-Prés," is one of the eleven short stories published in *I Wish Someone Were Waiting for Me Somewhere.*

"COURTING RITUALS OF THE SAINT-GERMAIN-DES-PRÉS"

Saint-Germain-des Prés? . . . I know what you're going to say: "God, that whole Left Bank thing is so clichéd. Françoise Sagan did it long before you, *chérie*—and sooo much better! Haven't you read *Bonjour Tristesse!*?"

SAINT-GERMAIN-DES-PRÉS

This area is named for the church that it surrounds—the former Abbey of Saint-Germain-des-Prés. After the Second World War, the Boulevard St. Germain became the intellectual and cultural site for Parisian life. Writers, intellectuals, and artists frequented the cafés, and it became the center of the existentialist movement with Jean-Paul Sartre and Simone de Beauvoir seen regularly in such cafés as les Deux Magots and Café de Flore.

I know.

But what do you expect? . . . I'm not sure any of this would've happened to me on Boulevard de Clichy or in some other part of Paris. That's just the way it is. *C'est la vie.*

So keep your thoughts to yourself and hear me out, because something tells me this story's going to amuse you. You love this kind of sentimental fluff—having someone make your heart beat faster with these evenings full of promise, these men who want you to think they're single and a little down on their luck.

I know you love it. It's perfectly normal. Still, you can't read Harlequin romances while you're sitting at café Lipp or Deux Magots. No, of course you can't.

THE BRASSERIE LIPP

By café Lipp, Gavalda is referring to the Brasserie Lipp, which opened in 1880 and sits across the street from the famous Café de Flore and Deux Magots. Other than briefly closing in the early 1900s for refurbishment, the café has remained open and popular in Paris for decades. Today, while pricey it isn't as expensive as the other two famous cafés, and literary and political figures still meet here for drinks.

So, this morning, I passed a man on Boulevard Saint-Germain. I was going up the street and he was coming down it. We were on the even-numbered side, which is more elegant.

I saw him coming from a distance. I don't know just what it was, maybe the carefree way he walked, or the way the skirt of his coat swung out in front of him . . . anyhow, I was twenty meters away and I already knew I couldn't go wrong.

Sure enough, when he passes, I see him look at me. I shoot him a mischievous smile—kind of like one of Cupid's arrows, only more discreet.

He smiles back.

I keep walking, still smiling, and think of Baudelaire's "To a Passerby." (What with that reference to Sagan earlier, by now you must have realized I'm what they call the literary type!) I slow down, trying to remember the lines of the poem . . . Tall, slender, in deep mourning . . . after that I don't know what . . . then . . . A woman passed, with a sumptuous hand, raising, dangling the embroidered hem . . . and at the end . . . O you whom I had loved, O you who knew it.

That gets me every time.

And during all this, pure and simple, I can sense this gaze of my Saint Sebastian (a reference to the arrow, see? Stay with me, okay?!) still on my back. It warms my shoulder blades deliciously, but I'd rather die than turn around. That would ruin the poem.

I'd stopped at the curb up by rue des Saints-Pères, watching the stream of cars for a chance to cross.

For the record: No self-respecting Parisienne on Boulevard Saint-Germain would ever cross on the white lines when the light is red. A self-respecting Parisienne watches the stream of cars and steps out, fully aware of the risk she's taking.

To die for the window display at Paulie Ka. Delicious.

I'm finally stepping out when a voice holds me back.

I'm not going to say, "a hot, virile voice" just to make you happy, because that's not how it was. Just a voice.

"Excuse me . . ."

I turn around. And who's there? . . . why, my scrumptious prey from a minute ago.

I might as well tell you right now, from that moment on: screw Baudelaire.

"I was wondering if you'd like to have dinner with me tonight. . . ."

In my head, I think, "How romantic. . ." But I answer:

"That's a little fast, don't you think?"

Without missing a beat, he says (and I swear this is the truth):

"Well, yes, I'll grant you that. But when I saw you walking away, I said to myself, 'This is ridiculous. Here's this woman I pass in the street. I smile at her, she smiles at me, we brush past one another, and we're about to lose each other. . . . It's ridiculous— no, really, it's absurd.'"

" . . ."

"What do you think? Does that seem like total nonsense to you, what I just said?"

"No, no, not at all."

I was beginning to feel a little uneasy. . . .

"Well, then? . . . What do you say? Let's say we meet here, tonight, at nine o'clock? Right at this spot."

Get ahold of yourself, girl. If you're going to have dinner with every man you smile at, you'll never get out of the gate. . . .

"Give me one good reason to say yes."

"One good reason. . . God . . . that's hard. . . ."

I watch him, amused.

And then, without warning, he takes my hand. "I think I've found a more or less suitable reason. . . ."

He passes my hand over his scruffy cheek.

"One good reason. There: Say yes so I'll have a reason to shave. . . . You know, I think I look a lot better when I've shaved."

And he gives me back my arm.

"Yes," I say.

"Good, then we're on! Can I walk you across the street? I don't want to lose you now."

This time I'm the one watching him walk off. He must be stroking his cheeks like a guy who's struck a good deal. . . . I'm sure he's enormously pleased with himself. He should be.

Late afternoon and a little nervous, I have to admit.

Beat at my own game. Should've read the rule book.

A little nervous, like a debutante having a bad-hair day.

A little nervous, like someone on the threshold of a love story.

At work, I answer the phone, I send faxes, I finish a mock-up for the photo researcher (what did you expect . . . a pretty, vivacious girl who sends faxes from Saint-Germain-des-Prés inevitably works in publishing. . .).

The tips of my fingers are ice-cold and everyone has to tell me everything twice.

Breathe, girl, breathe. . . .

At dusk, the street is quieter and the cars all have their headlights on.

The café tables are being brought in from the side-walks. There are people on the church square waiting to meet up with friends, and at the Beauregard people are lining up to see the latest Woody Allen film.

I don't want to be the first one there. It wouldn't be right. In fact, I decide to go a little late. Better to make him want me a little. So I go have a little pick-me-up to get the blood flowing back to my fingers.

Not at the Deux Magots, it's a little uncouth in the evenings—no one but fat American women on the lookout for the ghost of Simone de Beauvoir.

CAFÉ LES DEUX MAGOTS

Once frequented by Hemingway, Sartre, and Picasso, this famous café sits in a cluster of cafés in the heart of the chic Saint Germain-des-Prés. The café's name derives from two oriental statues in the dining area. Today, along with the entire area around it, this café is more popular than ever. More than its cuisine, the café's popularity is attributed to its alluring history and unbeatable location.

I take rue Saint-Benoît. The Chiquito will do just fine.

I push the door open, and right away there's the smell of beer and stale tobacco . . . the ding ding of the pinball machine . . . the hieratic bar owner with her dyed hair and my long blouse, support bra showing . . . the sound of the Vincennes night race playing in the background . . . some masons in stained overalls, putting off the hour of solitude or the old ball and chain . . . and the old regulars, fingers yellow, annoying everyone with their rents that haven't changed since '48. Bliss.

The men at the bar turn around from time to time and giggle among themselves like a bunch of schoolboys. My legs are in the aisle. They're very long. The aisle is kind of narrow and my skirt is very short. I see their stooped backs jiggling in fits and jerks.

I smoke a cigarette, sending the smoke out far in front of me. I stare off into space. Beautiful Day has won it in the final straight-away, ten-to-one odds, I learn.

I remember I've got *Kennedy and Me* in my bag, and I wonder if I wouldn't be better off staying here.

Salt pork with lentils and a half pitcher of rosé . . . wouldn't that be nice. . . .

But I pull myself together. You're there, over my shoulder, hop-ing for love (or less? or more? or not exactly?) with me, and I'm not going to leave you stranded with the owner of the Chiquito. That would be a little harsh.

I go out, cheeks rosy, and the cold whips my legs.

He's there, at the corner of rue des Saint-Pères, waiting for me. He sees me and walks over.

"I was worried—I was afraid you wouldn't come. I saw my reflection in a window, and I couldn't help but admire my cheeks, all nice and smooth. So I was worried."

"I'm sorry. I was waiting for the end of the Vincennes race and I lost track of time."

"Who won?"

"You bet?"

"No."

"Beautiful Day."

"Of course. I should've known." He smiles, taking my arm.

We walk in silence as far as rue Saint-Jacques. From time to time, he steals a look at me, examining my profile, but I know what he's really wondering just then is whether I'm wearing panty-hose or thigh highs.

Patience, my good man, patience. . . .

I'm going to take you to a place I really like."

I can picture it now . . . the kind of place where the waiters are relaxed but obsequious, smiling at him with a knowing air: "Good eeevening, monsieur . . . (*there she is then, the latest . . . you know, I liked the brunette from last time better . . .*) . . . the little table in the back as usual, monsieur? . . . bowing as he shows the way (*. . . but where does he dig up all these babes? . . .*), "May I take your coats? Veeery well."

He digs them up in the street, stupid.

But it's nothing like that.

He holds the door, letting me lead the way into a little wine bistro, and a bored-looking waiter asks us if we smoke. That's all.

He hung our things on a coatrack. In the half second he paused when he caught sight of the softness of my bust, I knew he didn't regret the little nick he'd given himself under the chin earlier when his hands betrayed him while he was shaving.

We drank extraordinary wine out of fat wineglasses. We are relatively subtle things, conceived precisely so as not to spoil the aroma of our nectars.

A bottle of Côte de Nuits, Gevrey-Chambertin 1986. Baby Jesus in velvet britches.

The man sitting across from me crinkles his eyes as he drinks.

I'm getting to know him better now.

He's wearing a gray cashmere turtleneck sweater. An old one. It's got elbow patches and a small tear near the right wrist. His twentieth birthday present, maybe . . . I can just see his mother, troubled by his disappointed pout telling him, "You won't be sorry, go ahead, try it on . . ." as she kisses him and strokes his back.

His jacket is unpretentious—it looks like any old tweed—but, as it's me and my lynx eyes, I can tell it's tailor-made. At Old England, the labels are bigger when the merchandise goes out straight from the Capucines workshops, and I saw the label when he leaned down to pick up his napkin.

His napkin that he'd dropped on purpose in order to settle once and for all this question of the pantyhose, I imagine.

He talks to me about a lot of things but never about himself. He always has a little trouble holding on to his train of thought when I let my fingers trail across my neck. He says, "And you?" and I don't ever talk about myself, either.

As we wait for dessert, my foot touches his ankle.

He puts his hand on mine and pulls it back suddenly because the sorbets have arrived.

He says something, but his words don't make a sound and I don't hear anything.

We're all worked up.

Horrors. His cell phone just rang.

As though they were one, all eyes in the restaurant fix on him as he deftly switches it off. He's certainly just wasted a lot of very good wine. Half-gulped mouthfuls caught in rasping throats. People choking, their fingers clenching knife handles or the creases of starched napkins.

Those damn things. There always has to be one, no matter where, no matter when.

The boor.

He's embarrassed. He's suddenly a little warm in his mommy's cashmere.

He nods his head at this group and that, as though to express his dismay. He looks at me and his shoulders have slumped a little.

"I'm sorry. . . ." He smiles at me again, but it's less self-assured, you could say.

I tell him, "It's no big deal. It's not like we're at the movies. Someday I'm going to kill someone. Some man or woman who answers the phone in the middle of the show. When you read it in the news brief, you'll know it was me. . . ."

"I will."

"You read the news briefs?"

"No. But I'm going to start, now that I have a chance of finding you there."

The sorbets were, how should I put it . . . delicious. Reinvigorated, my prince charming came to sit next to me when the coffee was served.

So, close that now he's sure: I'm wearing thigh highs.

He felt the little hook at the top of my thigh.

I know that at the moment, he doesn't know where he lives anymore.

He lifts my hair and kisses my neck, in the little hollow spot on the back.

He whispers into my ear that he loves Boulevard Saint-Germain, he loves burgundy and black currant sorbets.

I kiss his little cut. After all the time I've waited for this moment, I really get into it.

The coffee, the bill, the tip, our coats, all that is just details, details, details. Details that get in our way.

Our hearts are slamming against our chests.

He hands me my black coat and then . . .

I admire the work of the artists, hats off, it's very discreet, barely noticeable, it's very well calculated and perfectly executed: in placing the coat on my bare shoulders, proffered to him and soft as silk, he finds the half second necessary and the perfect tilt toward the inside pocket of his jacket to glance at the message screen on his cell phone.

I come to my senses. All at once.

Traitor.

Ingrate.

What in heaven's name were you thinking?!

What could possibly have distracted you when my shoulders were so round and warm and your hand was so close?!

What business was more important than my breasts offered to your view?

How could you let yourself be sidetracked while I was waiting for your breath on my back?

Couldn't you have waited to mess with the damn thing later, after you'd made love to me?

I button my coat all the way up.

In the street, I'm cold, I'm tired, and I feel sick.

I ask him to walk me to the nearest taxi stand.

He's in a panic.

Call 911, bud, you've got what you need.

But no. He's a stoic.

As if nothing has happened. As in, I'm walking a good friend to her taxi, I'm rubbing her sleeves to warm her and I'm chatting about the Paris night.

Classy almost to the end, I have to grant him that.

Before I climb into a black Mercedes taxi with Val-de-Marne plates, he says:

"But . . . we'll see each other again, won't we? I don't even know where you live. . . . Give me something, an address, a phone number. . . ."

He tears a scrap of paper out of his agenda and scribbles some numbers.

"Take this. The first number, that's home, the second, that's my cell, you can reach me there anytime. . . ."

That much I'd figured out.

Don't hesitate, no matter when, okay? . . . I'll be waiting to hear from you."

I WISH SOMEONE WERE WAITING FOR ME SOMEWHERE

I ask the driver to let me out at the top of the boulevard. I need to walk.

I kick some imaginary tin cans.
I hate cell phones, I hate Sagan, I hate Baudelaire and all those charlatans.
I hate my pride.

A Moveable Feast

BY ERNEST HEMINGWAY (1964)

Born in 1899 in Oak Park, Illinois, a suburb of Chicago, Ernest Hemingway lived with his family in Illinois until he graduated from high school and headed to Kansas City for a career in journalism. He went to work for the *Kansas City Star*, but left his job after only a few months in order to join the Red Cross Ambulance Services. (Poor vision kept him out of the military.) Much of his early work is based on his experiences in Italy as an ambulance driver and upon his return to America, he wrote prolifically.

163 — PARIS — Le Café de la Paix. - Boulevard des Capucines A. P
The Café de la Paix - Corner of the Place of the Opera

Café de la Paix, 1919

Though he was known for his adventurous lifestyle, he was a disciplined writer who woke before dawn every morning to write. He wrote fondly of Paris, but never seemed to feel completely at home there the way he did in Cuba and Idaho. Hemingway lived in Paris through the 1920s with other expatriates now commonly referred to as the Lost Generation. Fitzgerald and Stein were among his closest friends during this time of his life. He married three times and had three sons.

In July of 1961, just three weeks shy of his sixty-second birthday, Hemingway committed suicide in his home in Ketchum, Idaho.

Known for his minimalist style, Hemingway provides us with only as much as we need, thereby allowing us to make the story our own. He credits his writing style to his on-the-job-training at the *Kansas City Star*. "Use short sentences. Use short first paragraphs. Use vigorous English. Be positive, not negative." He received the Pulitzer Prize in 1953 for *The Old Man and the Sea* and the Nobel Prize in Literature in 1954. He first depicts life in Paris through his novel, *The Sun Also Rises*, published in 1926. *A Moveable Feast* is set in the 1920s when so many Americans went to Paris after the First World War, however, the memoir was written in the 1950s while he lived in Idaho.

FROM CHAPTER ONE, "A GOOD CAFÉ ON THE PLACE ST. MICHEL"

Then there was the bad weather. It would come in one day when the fall was over. We would have to shut the windows in the night against the rain and the cold wind would strip the leaves from the trees in the Place Contrescarpe.

(LA) PLACE DE LA CONTRESCARPE

A small square in the southern part of the city, with a large and rich history. In the sixteenth century a group of writers known as La Pléiade (named after the constellation) used to meet here. There is also a memorial plaque to the old "pine-cone club" immortalized in the writings of Rabelais. The square has always been a popular gathering place for festivals, especially Bastille Day. It's one of the liveliest areas in Paris on the weekends.

The leaves lay sodden in the rain and the wind drove the rain against the big green autobus at the terminal and the Café des Amateurs was crowded and the windows misted over from the heat and the smoke inside. It was a sad, evilly run café where the drunkards of the quarter crowded together and I kept away from it because of the smell of dirty bodies and the sour smell of drunkenness. The men and women who frequented the Amateurs stayed drunk all of the time, or all of the time they could afford it, mostly on wine which they bought by the half-liter or liter. Many strangely named apéritifs were advertised, but few people could afford them except as a foundation to build their wine drunks on. The women drunkards were called *poivrottes* which meant female rummies.

The Café des Amateurs was the cesspool of the rue Mouffetard, the wonderful narrow crowded market street which led into the Place Contrescarpe.

RUE MOUFFETARD

This is one of Paris's oldest and most historically interesting streets. It has been a major roadway since Roman times. In the seventeenth and eighteenth centuries the street was called Grande Rue du Faubourg St.-Marcel meaning "street of the suburb Saint-Marceau." Even now, many shops have ancient painted signs. Practically every building along this street has a story worth knowing.

The squat toilets of the old apartment houses, one by the side of the stairs on each floor with the two cleated cement shoe-shaped elevations on each side of the aperture so a *locataire* would not slip, emptied into cesspools which were emptied by pumping into horse-drawn tank wagons at night. In the summer time, with all windows open, we would hear the pumping and the odor was very strong. The tank wagons were painted brown and saffron color and in the moonlight when they worked on the rue Cardinal Lemoine their wheeled, horse-drawn cylinders looked like Braque paintings. No one emptied the Café des Amateurs though, and its yellowed poster stating the terms and penalties of the law against public drunkenness was as flyblown and disregarded as its clients were constant and ill-smelling.

All of the sadness of the city came suddenly with the first cold rains of winter, and there were no more tops to the high white houses as you walked but only the wet blackness of the street and the closed doors of the small shops, the herb sellers, the stationery and the newspaper shops, the midwife—second class—and the hotel where Verlaine had died where I had a room on the top floor where I worked.

It was either six or eight flights up to the top floor and it was very cold and I knew how much it would cost for a bundle of small twigs, three wire-wrapped packets of short, half-pencil length pieces of split pine to catch fire from the twigs, and then the bundle of half-dried lengths of hard wood that I must buy to make a fire that would warm the room. So I went to the far side of the street to look up at the roof in the rain and see if any chimneys were going, and how the smoke blew. There was no smoke and I thought about how the chimney would be cold and might not draw and of the room possibly filling with smoke, and the fuel wasted, and the money gone with it, and I walked on in the rain.

LYCÉE HENRI IV (QUATRE)

The Lycée Henri IV (Quatre) is a public secondary school located on the left bank in an area referred to as the Latin Quarter. The school has one of the most challenging curriculums and is considered one of the most prestigious schools in all of France.

I walked down past the Lycée Henri Quatre and the ancient church of St.-Etienne-du-Mont and the windswept Place du Panthéon and cut in for shelter to the right and finally came out on the lee side of the Boulevard St.-Michel and worked on down it past the Cluny and the Boulevard St.-Germain until I came to a good café that I knew on the Place St.-Michel.

ST-ETIENNE-DU-MONT

This church is home to both the shrine of Saint Geneviève, patron saint of Paris, and the remains of two literary giants—Racine and Pascal. The construction of the building spanned two centuries from 1492 to 1626 and is gothic in style, which was unusual for its time. The tomb of Saint Geneviève was destroyed during the Revolution, but her relics were gathered and are now honored here. The stained glass windows are breathtaking and alone are reason enough to visit.

It was a pleasant café, warm and clean and friendly, and I hung up my old waterproof on the coat rack to dry and put my worn and weathered felt hat on the rack above the bench and ordered a *café au lait*. The waiter brought it and I took out a notebook from the pocket of the coat and a pencil and started to write. I was writing about up in Michigan and since it was a wild, cold, blowing day it was that sort of day in the story. I had already seen the end of fall come through boyhood, youth and young manhood, and in one place you could write about it better than in another. That was called transplanting yourself, I thought, and it could be as necessary with people as with other sorts of growing things. But in the story the boys were drinking and this made me thirsty and I ordered a rum St. James. This tasted wonderful on the cold day and I kept on writing feeling very well and feeling the good Martinique rum warm me all through my body and my spirit.

A girl came in the café and sat by herself at a table near the window. She was very pretty with a face fresh as a newly minted coin if they minted coins in smooth flesh with rain-freshened skin, and her hair was black as a crow's wing and cut sharply and diagonally across her cheek.

I looked at her and she disturbed me and made me very excited. I wished I could put her in the story, or anywhere, but she had placed herself so she could watch the street and the entry and I knew she was waiting for someone. So I went on writing.

The story was writing itself and I was having a hard time keeping up with it. I ordered another rum St. James and I watched the girl whenever I looked up, or when I sharpened my pencil with a pencil sharpener with the shavings curling into the saucer under my drink.

I've seen you, beauty, and you belong to me now, whoever you are waiting for and if I never see you again, I thought. You belong to me and all Paris belongs to me and I belong to this notebook and this pencil.

Then I went back to writing and I entered far into the story and was lost in it. I was writing it now and it was not writing itself and I did not look up nor know anything about the time nor think where I was nor order any more rum St. James. I was tired of rum St. James without thinking about it. Then the story was finished and I was very tired. I read the last paragraph and then I looked up and looked for the girl and she had gone. I hope she's gone with a good man, I thought. But I felt sad.

Reprinted with the permission of Scribner, a Division of Simon & Schuster, Inc. from *A Moveable Feast* by Ernest Hemingway. Copyright © 1964 by Mary Hemingway. Copyright renewed © 1992 by John H. Hemingway, Patrick Hemingway and Gregory Hemingway.

PARIS.
L'Arc de Triomphe
de l'Étoile.

L'Arc de Triomphe de l'Etoile, 1909

Les Misérables

BY VICTOR HUGO (1862)

Victor Hugo, thought to be one of the most important French Romantic writers of the nineteenth century and one of the most influential French writers of all time, was born in Besançon, France in 1802. He was only fourteen when he wrote his first play and at fifteen he won a poetry award from l'Academie Française. Five years later, he published his first book of poems, *Odes et Poésies Diverses*. In 1822, he married Adele Foucher.

It is practically impossible to talk about Hugo without discussing his politics. His writing and political beliefs intermingled and his views shifted over the course of his life. He was an active supporter of the Monarchy, but later became a Republican and opposed the 1848 coup d'etat by Napoléon III. His opposition led to his exile in 1851. Hugo lived in the Channel Islands until 1870 when he was finally allowed to return to France. Six years later, he was elected to the senate. He lived near the Abbey of Saint-Germain-des-Prés cathedral and led the effort to restore the church to its former glory. After such extensive restoration the church is arguably among the most beautiful buildings in Paris.

Nothing that occurred in his life weakened his writing, in fact, such events seemed to strengthen his will and hone his craft. He was such a force in France that upon his death in 1885 his body lay in state underneath the Arc de Triomphe before being buried at the Panthéon.

Though most of his earlier work has been largely overshadowed by his great novels, Hugo demonstrated at an early age the desire to throw out the rules of classical writing and use sounds and lyricism to create his own style. In addition to creating his own style, he had his own agenda. An ongoing theme in his work is man's never ending struggle between good and evil, particularly as it relates to the daily suffering he saw among people in his own city. His first great novel was *Notre-Dame de Paris*, published in 1831. When the book was published in English the title was changed to *The Hunchback of Notre Dame* in order to emphasize the main character. *Les Misérables*, his second great work published in 1862, is set in the underground world of nineteenth century Paris over a twenty year period that includes the Napoleonic wars. When asked why he wrote *Les Misérables*, Hugo replied, "I condemn slavery, I banish poverty, I teach ignorance, I treat disease, I lighten the night, and I hate hatred. That is what I am, and that is why I have written *Les Misérables*."

In this portion of *Les Misérables*, Jean Valjean, an ex-convict who spent nineteen years in jail for stealing a loaf of bread and for trying but failing to escape, has just buried his money in the woods and taken refuge in an old house in Paris with the hopes of disappearing in the Parisian crowds.

FROM VOLUME II, BOOK FOUR, "THE GORBEAU HOVEL," CHAPTER ONE

Forty years ago, a rambler who had ventured into that unknown country of the Salpetriere, and who had mounted to the Barriere d'Italie by way of the boulevard, reached a point where it might be said that Paris disappeared. It was no longer solitude, for there were passers-by; it was not the country, for there were houses and streets; it was not the city, for the streets had ruts like highways, and the grass grew in them; it was not a village, the houses were too lofty. What was it, then? It was an inhabited place where there was nobody. It was a desert place where there was somebody. It was a boulevard of the great city, a street of Paris, wilder at night than a forest and gloomier by day than a graveyard. It was the old quarter of the horse-market.

It was the old quarter of the Marche-aux-Chevaux.

The rambler, if he risked himself outside the four decrepit walls of this Marche-aux-Chevaux; if he consented even to pass beyond the Rue du Petit-Banquier, after leaving on his right a garden protected by high walls; then a field in which tan-bark mills rose like gigantic beaver huts; then an enclosure encumbered with timber, with a heap of stumps, sawdust, and shavings, on which stood a large dog, barking; then a long, low, utterly dilapidated wall, with a little black door in mourning, laden with mosses, which were covered with flowers in the spring; then, in the most deserted spot, a frightful and decrepit building, on which ran the inscription in large letters: POST NO BILLS,—this daring rambler would have reached little known latitudes at the corner of the Rue des Vignes-Saint-Marcel. There, near a factory, and between two garden walls, there could be seen, at that epoch, a mean building, which, at the first glance, seemed as small as a thatched hovel, and which was, in reality, as large as a cathedral. It presented its side and gable to the public road; hence its apparent diminutiveness. Nearly the whole of the house was hidden. Only the door and one window could be seen.

This hovel was only one story high.

The first detail that struck the observer was, that the door could never have been anything but the door of a hovel, while the window, if it had been carved out of dressed stone instead of being in rough masonry, might have been the lattice of a lordly mansion.

The door was nothing but a collection of worm-eaten planks roughly bound together by cross-beams which resembled roughly hewn logs. It opened directly on a steep staircase of lofty steps, muddy, chalky, plaster-stained, dusty steps, of the same width as itself, which could be seen from the street, running straight up like a ladder and disappearing in the darkness between two walls. The top of the shapeless bay into which this door shut was masked by a narrow scantling in the centre of which a triangular hole had been sawed, which served both as wicket and air-hole when the door was closed. On the inside of the door the figures 52 had been traced with a couple of strokes of a brush dipped in ink, and above the scantling the same hand had daubed the number 50, so that one hesitated. Where was one? Above the door it said, "Number 50"; the inside replied, "no, Number 52." No one knows what dust-colored figures were suspended like draperies from the triangular opening.

The window was large, sufficiently elevated, garnished with Venetian blinds, and with a frame in large square panes; only these large panes were suffering from various wounds, which were both concealed and betrayed by an ingenious paper bandage. And the blinds, dislocated and unpasted, threatened passers-by rather than screened the occupants.

The horizontal slats were missing here and there and had been naively replaced with boards nailed on perpendicularly; so that what began as a blind ended as a shutter. This door with an unclean, and this window with an honest though dilapidated air, thus beheld on the same house, produced the effect of two incomplete beggars walking side by side, with different miens beneath the same rags, the one having always been a mendicant, and the other having once been a gentleman.

The staircase led to a very vast edifice which resembled a shed which had been converted into a house. This edifice had, for its intestinal tube, a long corridor, on which opened to right and left sorts of compartments of varied dimensions which were inhabitable under stress of circumstances, and rather more like stalls than cells. These chambers received their light from the vague waste grounds in the neighborhood.

All this was dark, disagreeable, wan, melancholy, sepulchral; traversed according as the crevices lay in the roof or in the door, by cold rays or by icy winds. An interesting and picturesque peculiarity of this sort of dwelling is the enormous size of the spiders.

To the left of the entrance door, on the boulevard side, at about the height of a man from the ground, a small window which had been walled up formed a square niche full of stones which the children had thrown there as they passed by.

A portion of this building has recently been demolished. From what still remains of it one can form a judgment as to what it was in former days. As a whole, it was not over a hundred years old. A hundred years is youth in a church and age in a house. It seems as though man's lodging partook of his ephemeral character, and God's house of his eternity.

The postmen called the house Number 50-52; but it was known in the neighborhood as the Gorbeau house.

Let us explain whence this appellation was derived.

Collectors of petty details, who become herbalists of anecdotes, and prick slippery dates into their memories with a pin, know that there was in Paris, during the last century, about 1770, two attorneys at the Chatelet named, one Corbeau (Raven), the other Renard (Fox). The two names had been forestalled by La Fontaine. The opportunity was too fine for the lawyers; they made the most of it. A parody was immediately put in circulation in the galleries of the court-house, in verses that limped a little:

Maitre Corbeau, sur un dossier perche,
Tenait dans son bee une saisie executoire;
Maitre Renard, par l'odeur alleche,
Lui fit a peu pres cette histoire:
He! bonjour. Etc.

The two honest practitioners, embarrassed by the jests, and finding the bearing of their heads interfered with by the shouts of laughter which followed them, resolved to get rid of their names, and hit upon the expedient of applying to the king.

Their petition was presented to Louis XV on the same day when the Papal Nuncio, on the one hand, and the Cardinal de la Roche-Aymon on the other, both devoutly kneeling, were each engaged in putting on, in his Majesty's presence, a slipper on the bare feet of Madame du Barry, who had just got out of bed. The king, who was laughing, continued to laugh, passed gayly from the two bishops to the two lawyers, and bestowed on these limbs of the law their former names, or nearly so. By the king's command, Maitre Corbeau was permitted to add a tail to his initial letter and to call himself Gorbeau. Maitre Renard was less lucky; all he obtained was leave to place a P in front of his R, and to call himself Prenard; so that the second name bore almost as much resemblance as the first.

Now, according to local tradition, this Maitre Gorbeau had been the proprietor of the building numbered 50-52 on the Boulevard de l'Hopital. He was even the author of the monumental window.

Hence the edifice bore the name of the Gorbeau house.

Opposite this house, among the trees of the boulevard, rose a great elm which was three-quarters dead; almost directly facing it opens the Rue de la Barrière des Gobelins, a street then without houses, unpaved, planted with unhealthy trees, which was green or muddy according to the season, and which ended squarely in the exterior wall of Paris. An odor of copperas issued in puffs from the roofs of the neighboring factory.

RUE DE LA BARRIÈRE DES GOBELINS

This area was named for a dye works founded by Jean Gobelin in the middle of the fifteenth century. In 1662, Louis XIV purchased the Gobelins factory and an upholstery factory was also established, which included designs in both tapestry and furniture. The business closed in

---

1694 due to financial problems, but reopened three years later. Business was once again halted due to the French Revolution, and revived in 1826. The operation is still running today and guided tours are given.

The barrier was close at hand. In 1823 the city wall was still in existence.

This barrier itself evoked gloomy fancies in the mind. It was the road to Bicetre. It was through it that, under the Empire and the Restoration, prisoners condemned to death re-entered Paris on the day of their execution. It was there, that, about 1829, was committed that mysterious assassination, called "The assassination of the Fontainebleau barrier," whose authors justice was never able to discover; a melancholy problem which has never been elucidated, a frightful enigma which has never been unriddled. Take a few steps, and you come upon that fatal Rue Croulebarbe, where Ulbach stabbed the goat-girl of Ivry to the sound of thunder, as in the melodramas. A few paces more, and you arrive at the abominable pollarded elms of the Barriere Saint-Jacques, that expedient of the philanthropist to conceal the scaffold, that miserable and shameful Place de Grove of a shop-keeping and bourgeois society, which recoiled before the death penalty, neither daring to abolish it with grandeur, nor to uphold it with authority.

Leaving aside this Place Saint-Jacques, which was, as it were, predestined, and which has always been horrible, probably the most mournful spot on that mournful boulevard, seven and thirty years ago, was the spot which even to-day is so unattractive, where stood the building Number 50-52.

Bourgeois houses only began to spring up there twenty-five years later. The place was unpleasant. In addition to the gloomy thoughts which assailed one there, one was conscious of being between the Salpetriere, a glimpse of whose dome could be seen, and Bicetre, whose outskirts one was fairly touching; that is to say, between the madness of women and the madness of men.

THE SALPÊTRIÈRE

Originally a gunpowder factory, the Salpêtrière became a prison for prostitutes, the criminally insane, and those with epilepsy. In 1656, Louis XIV decided to turn the building into a hospital. In the 1800s Dr. Jean Martin Charcot, often referred to as the father of neurology, made the hospital famous for its work in psychiatry. Students worldwide came to the Salpêtrière to learn from Charcot. Among his students was Sigmund Freud. Today, the Pitié-Salpêtrière is a teaching hospital with departments in most medical fields. It is one of the largest hospitals in Europe.

As far as the eye could see, one could perceive nothing but the abattoirs, the city wall, and the fronts of a few factories, resembling barracks or monasteries; everywhere about stood hovels, rubbish, ancient walls blackened like cerecloths, new white walls like winding-sheets; everywhere parallel rows of trees, buildings erected on a line, flat constructions, long, cold rows, and the melancholy sadness of right angles. Not an unevenness of the ground, not a caprice in the architecture, not a fold. The ensemble was glacial, regular, hideous. Nothing oppresses the heart like symmetry. It is because symmetry is ennui, and ennui is at the very foundation of grief. Despair yawns. Something more terrible than a hell where one suffers may be imagined, and that is a hell where one is bored. If such a hell existed, that bit of the Boulevard de l'Hopital might have formed the entrance to it.

Nevertheless, at nightfall, at the moment when the daylight is vanishing, especially in winter, at the hour when the twilight breeze tears from the elms their last russet leaves, when the darkness is deep and starless, or when the moon and the wind are making openings in the clouds and losing themselves in the shadows, this boulevard suddenly becomes frightful. The black lines sink inwards and are lost in the shades, like morsels of the infinite. The passer-by cannot refrain from recalling the innumerable traditions of the place which are connected with the gibbet. The solitude of this spot, where so many crimes have been committed, had something terrible about it. One almost had a presentiment of meeting with traps in that darkness; all the confused forms of the darkness seemed suspicious, and the long, hollow square, of which one caught a glimpse between each tree, seemed graves: by day it was ugly; in the evening melancholy; by night it was sinister.

In summer, at twilight, one saw, here and there, a few old women seated at the foot of the elm, on benches mouldy with rain. These good old women were fond of begging.

However, this quarter, which had a superannuated rather than an antique air, was tending even then to transformation. Even at that time any one who was desirous of seeing it had to make haste. Each day some detail of the whole effect was disappearing. For the last twenty years the station of the Orleans railway has stood beside the old faubourg and distracted it, as it does to-day. Wherever it is placed on the borders of a capital, a railway station is the death of a suburb and the birth of a city. It seems as though, around these great centres of the movements of a people, the earth, full of germs, trembled and yawned, to engulf the ancient dwellings of men and to allow new ones to spring forth, at the rattle of these powerful machines, at the breath of these monstrous horses of civilization which devour coal and vomit fire. The old houses crumble and new ones rise.

Since the Orleans railway has invaded the region of the Salpetriere, the ancient, narrow streets which adjoin the moats Saint-Victor and the Jardin des Plantes tremble, as they are violently traversed three or four times each day by those currents of coach fiacres and omnibuses which, in a given time, crowd back the houses to the right and the left; for there are things which are odd when said that are rigorously exact; and just as it is true to say that in large cities the sun makes the southern fronts of houses to vegetate and grow, it is certain that the frequent passage of vehicles enlarges streets.

JARDIN DES PLANTES

This botanical garden created in 1626 by Guy La Brosse and Jean Herouard, physicians to Louis XIII, began as a royal medicinal herb garden. It was opened to the public in 1640. The garden sits on the Left Bank of the Seine and includes the Natural History Museum, a small zoo, and a botany school. With its tropical hothouse, alpine garden, rose garden, and Art Deco-style winter garden, it is France's most popular botanical garden.

The symptoms of a new life are evident. In this old provincial quarter, in the wildest nooks, the pavement shows itself, the sidewalks begin to crawl and to grow longer, even where there are as yet no pedestrians. One morning,—a memorable morning in July, 1845,—black pots of bitumen were seen smoking there; on that day it might be said that civilization had arrived in the Rue de l'Ourcine, and that Paris had entered the suburb of Saint-Marceau.

Le Grand Palais, 1909

The Ambassadors

BY HENRY JAMES (1903)

Henry James was born in 1843 and raised by a wealthy family in New York City. He traveled back and forth between Europe and America throughout his childhood and lived in Paris for a year when he was twelve. He attended Harvard Law School briefly, but decided instead on a life of writing. He went on to write twenty-two novels, novellas, travelogues, short stories, and essays. He moved to Paris in 1875 and lived at 29 rue Camdon while working as a contributor for the *New York Tribune*, and writing his first novel, *The American* (1877). While he described Paris as "irresistible" he found himself missing London, so he lived most of his life in London and visited Paris often. James never married, but he was by no means a hermit. He was invited to and attended dinner parties often and he felt most at home among the highest society circles.

Angry at the United States for not entering World War I at the start, he renounced his citizenship in 1915 and became a citizen of Great Britain. Later that same year, he had a stroke. He never recovered and died in February 1916.

Whether it was a novel or a travelogue, James's work dealt with the impact of Europeans on Americans. In his earlier works, most notably *Portrait of a Lady*, James's style was simple, yet he was unafraid to experiment with form and structure. His use of long sentences has been both criticized and praised. His subtle humor was especially unusual and perhaps is appreciated more today. He did not, however, experiment with narrative, choosing to tell his stories through the commonly used omniscient point of view. With several novels to his name, he decided to take a break from the genre and focus on short stories and plays. When he did finally return to the novel, he did not rely on the simple, direct approach; instead he used complex double imagery and sentences so long that one paragraph would sometimes go on for one or two full pages. It is understandable for a reader to feel bogged down by James's detailed descriptions and frustrated with the effort it takes to follow his prose. That said, few authors have been able to write about the nature of people and the dynamics of relationships in such an entertaining and timeless fashion as Henry James.

Written in 1903 while he was living in England, *The Ambassadors* was James's final and perhaps most complex piece of work.

In the novel, Lambert Strether has traveled to Paris with the hope of persuading his widowed fiancée's supposedly wayward son to return home and become part of the family business, but of course, there are complications. The novel is told entirely in third person from Strether's point of view and focuses on the consciousness of the characters. As with all of James's novels, the reader must pay close attention because the humor is low-key but insightful and the plot grows complicated rather quickly; James was quoted in the *New York Edition* as saying that he considered *The Ambassadors* among his finest works.

FROM PART ONE, CHAPTER FIVE

Strether called, his second morning in Paris, on the bankers of the Rue Scribe to whom his letter of credit was addressed, and he made this visit attended by Waymarsh, in whose company he had crossed from London two days before. They had hastened to the Rue Scribe on the morrow of their arrival, but Strether had not then found the letters the hope of which prompted this errand. He had had as yet none at all; hadn't expected them in London, but had counted on several in Paris, and, disconcerted now, had presently strolled back to the Boulevard with a sense of injury that he felt himself taking for as good a start as any other. It would serve, this spur to his spirit, he reflected, as, pausing at the top of the street, he looked up and down the great foreign avenue, it would serve to begin business with. His idea was to begin business immediately, and it did much for him the rest of his day that the beginning of business awaited him. He did little else till night but ask himself what he should do if he hadn't fortunately had so much to do; but he put himself the question in many different situations and connexions. What carried him hither and yon was an admirable theory that nothing he could do wouldn't be in some manner related to what he fundamentally had on hand, or would be—should he happen to have a scruple—wasted for it. He did happen to have a scruple—a scruple about taking no definite step till he should get letters; but this reasoning carried it off. A single day to feel his feet—he had felt them as yet only at Chester and in London—was he could consider, none too much; and having, as he had often privately expressed it, Paris to reckon with, he threw these hours of freshness consciously into the reckoning. They made it continually greater, but that was what it had best be if it was to be anything at all, and he gave himself up till far into the evening, at the theatre and on the return, after the theatre, along the bright congested Boulevard, to feeling it grow. Waymarsh had accompanied him this time to the play, and the two men had walked together, as a first stage, from the Gymnase to the Café Riche, into the crowded "terrace" of which establishment—the night, or rather the morning, for midnight had struck, being bland and populous—they had wedged themselves for refreshment.

CAFÉ RICHE

Café Riche was a famous and chic gathering place in its time. Located on the Boulevard des Italiens, it came and went along with its surroundings. The French as well as foreigners patronized the café. In Guy de Maupassant's *Bel Ami*, he sets a scene at Café Riche and takes his time describing the place in detail as it was during his time.

Waymarsh, as a result of some discussion with his friend, had made a marked virtue of his having now let himself go; and there had been elements of impression in their half-hour over their watered beer-glasses that gave him his occasion for conveying that he held this compromise with his stiffer self to have become extreme. He conveyed it—for it was still, after all, his stiffer self who gloomed out of the glare of the terrace—in solemn silence; and there was indeed a great deal of critical silence, every way, between the companions, even till they gained the Place de l'Opera, as to the character of their nocturnal progress.

This morning there were letters—letters which had reached London, apparently all together, the day of Strether's journey, and had taken their time to follow him; so that, after a controlled impulse to go into them in the reception-room of the bank, which, reminding him of the post-office at Woollett, affected him as the abutment of some transatlantic bridge, he slipped them into the pocket of his loose grey overcoat with a sense of the felicity of carrying them off. Waymarsh, who had had letters yesterday, had had them again to-day, and Waymarsh suggested in this particular no controlled impulses. The last one he was at all events likely to be observed to struggle with was clearly that of bringing to a premature close any visit to the Rue Scribe.

Strether had left him there yesterday; he wanted to see the papers, and he had spent, by what his friend could make out, a succession of hours with the papers. He spoke of the establishment, with emphasis, as a post of superior observation; just as he spoke generally of his actual damnable doom as a device for hiding from him what was going on. Europe was best described, to his mind, as an elaborate engine for dissociating the confined American from that indispensable knowledge, and was accordingly only rendered bearable by these occasional stations of relief, traps for the arrest of wandering western airs. Strether, on his side, set himself to walk again—he had his relief in his pocket; and indeed, much as he had desired his budget, the growth of restlessness might have been marked in him from the moment he had assured himself of the superscription of most of the missives it contained. This restlessness became therefore his temporary law; he knew he should recognise as soon as see it the best place of all for settling down with his chief correspondent. He had for the next hour an accidental air of looking for it in the windows of shops; he came down the Rue de la Paix in the sun and, passing across the Tuileries and the river, indulged more than once—as if on finding himself determined—in a sudden pause before the book-stalls of the opposite quay.

HÔTEL WESTMINSTER

Henry James lived, with his parents, in the Hôtel Westminster at 13 rue de la Paix for a while when he was twelve. Today, the posh boutique hotel, named after the Duke of Westminster who lived in Paris for some time, would most likely suit the James family's high standards and impeccable taste. The hotel stands at the same address, near the Louvre, the Opéra, the Tuileries Garden, and Place Vendôme, a square at the north end of the Tuileries. James's familiarity and fondness with this area of Paris is seen in his work.

In the garden of the Tuileries he had lingered, on two or three spots, to look; it was as if the wonderful Paris spring had stayed him as he roamed.

TUILERIES GARDEN

This garden remains, for the most part, as it was when it was originally planned in 1664. It is surrounded by the Louvre to the east, the Seine to the south, the Place de la Concorde to the west, and the rue de Rivoli to the north.

The prompt Paris morning struck its cheerful notes—in a soft breeze and a sprinkled smell, in the light flit, over the garden-floor, of bareheaded girls with the buckled strap of oblong boxes, in the type of ancient thrifty persons basking betimes where terrace-walls were warm, in the blue-frocked brass-labelled officialism of humble rakers and scrapers, in the deep references of a straight-pacing priest or the sharp ones of a white-gaitered red-legged soldier. He watched little brisk figures, figures whose movement was as the tick of the great Paris clock, take their smooth diagonal from point to point; the air had a taste as of something mixed with art, something that presented nature as a white-capped master-chef. The palace was gone, Strether remembered the palace; and when he gazed into the irremediable void of its site the historic sense in him might have been freely at play—the play under which in Paris indeed it so often winces like a touched nerve. He filled out spaces with dim symbols of scenes; he caught the gleam of white statues at the base of which, with his letters out, he could tilt back a straw-bottomed chair. But his drift was, for reasons, to the other side, and it floated him unspent up the Rue de Seine and as far as the Luxembourg.

THE LUXEMBOURG GARDENS

The Luxembourg Gardens came about following Henri IV's assassination in 1610. Haunted by his memory, Henri's wife, Marie de Medicis, could not continue living in the Louvre so she had the Palais du Luxembourg and the surrounding gardens built to look like her childhood home, Florence's Palazzo Pitti. The Gardens were completed in 1625.

In the Luxembourg Gardens he pulled up; here at last he found his nook, and here, on a penny chair from which terraces, alleys, vistas, fountains, little trees in green tubs, little women in white caps and shrill little girls at play all sunnily "composed" together, he passed an hour in which the cup of his impressions seemed truly to overflow.

THE LUXEMBOURG GARDENS TODAY

The Luxembourg Gardens has been open to the public since the seventeenth century and is one of the most successful parks in the world because it's located in the heart of the city thereby making it easy to get to from any direction. The park attracts families, students, and older adults. Visitors can sign up for tennis, and children can ride a pony, go to a puppet theater and rent toy sailboats. The public is even welcome to sit in on a hearing of the French Senate.

But a week had elapsed since he quitted the ship, and there were more things in his mind than so few days could account for. More than once, during the time, he had regarded himself as admonished; but the admonition this morning was formidably sharp. It took as it hadn't done yet the form of a question—the question of what he was doing with such an extraordinary sense of escape. This sense was sharpest after he had read his letters, but that was also precisely why the question pressed. Four of the letters were from Mrs. Newsome and none of them short; she had lost no time, had followed on his heels while he moved, so expressing herself that he now could measure the probable frequency with which he should hear. They would arrive, it would seem, her communications, at the rate of several a week; he should be able to count, it might even prove, on more than one by each mail. If he had begun yesterday with a small grievance he had therefore an opportunity to begin to-day with its opposite. He read the letters successively and slowly, putting others back into his pocket but keeping these for a long time afterwards gathered in his lap. He held them there, lost in thought, as if to prolong the presence of what they gave him; or as if at the least to assure them their part in the constitution of some lucidity.

His friend wrote admirably, and her tone was even more in her style than in her voice—he might almost, for the hour, have had to come this distance to get its full carrying quality; yet the plenitude of his consciousness of difference consorted perfectly with the deepened intensity of the connexion. It was the difference, the difference of being just where he was and as he was, that formed the escape—this difference was so much greater than he had dreamed it would be; and what he finally sat there turning over was the strange logic of his finding himself so free. He felt it in a manner his duty to think out his state, to approve the process, and when he came in fact to trace the steps and add up the items they sufficiently accounted for the sum. He had never expected—that was the truth of it—again to find himself young, and all the years and other things it had taken to make him so were exactly his present arithmetic. He had to make sure of them to put his scruple to rest.

It all sprang at bottom from the beauty of Mrs. Newsome's desire that he should be worried with nothing that was not of the essence of his task; by insisting that he should thoroughly intermit and break she had so provided for his freedom that she would, as it were, have only herself to thank. Strether could not at this point indeed have completed his thought by the image of what she might have to thank herself for: the image, at best, of his own likeness—poor Lambert Strether washed up on the sunny strand by the waves of a single day, poor Lambert Strether thankful for breathing-time and stiffening himself while he gasped. There he was, and with nothing in his aspect or his posture to scandalise: it was only true that if he had seen Mrs. Newsome coming he would instinctively have jumped up to walk away a little. He would have come round and back to her bravely, but he would have had first to pull himself together. She abounded in news of the situation at home, proved to him how perfectly she was arranging for his absence, told him who would take up this and who take up that exactly where he had left it, gave him in fact chapter and verse for the moral that nothing would suffer. It filled for him, this tone of hers, all the air; yet it struck him at the same time as the hum of vain things. This latter effect was what he tried to justify—and with the success that, grave though the appearance, he at last lighted on a form that was happy. He arrived at it by the inevitable recognition of his having been a fortnight before one of the weariest of men. If ever a man had come off tired Lambert Strether was that man; and hadn't it been distinctly on the ground of his fatigue that his wonderful friend at home had so felt for him and so contrived? It seemed to him somehow at these instants that, could he only maintain with sufficient firmness his grasp of that truth, it might become in a manner his compass and his helm. What he wanted most was some idea that would simplify, and nothing would do this so much as the fact that he was done for and finished. If it had been in such a light that he had just detected in his cup the dregs of youth, that was a mere flaw of the surface of his scheme. He was so distinctly fagged-out that it must serve precisely as his convenience, and if he could but consistently be good for little enough he might do everything he wanted.

Partie de la Grand Salle Restaurant, 1905

Satori in Paris

BY JACK KEROUAC (1966)

When Jack Kerouac was born in 1922 in Lowell, Massachusetts, his parents had just moved to the United States from Quebec, Canada, in search of work. He did not learn to speak English until he was six years old, since the dialect of French called Joual was the only language spoken in his home. He earned a football scholarship to Columbia University, but he lacked the patience or discipline a university required and he dropped out. He stayed in New York however, and became friends with a group of writers that would eventually be known as the Beats. He drank heavily throughout his life and married three times, but he never stopped writing. While depressed and self-medicating with alcohol and drugs, he still managed to write. *The Subterraneans* and *Desolation Angels* were two of the novels he wrote during this time.

After his divorce from Joan Haverty in 1951, he began traveling extensively throughout the country and into Mexico. In 1954 he became interested in Buddhism, but he was never able to give up the hard-drinking life he had become so accustomed to living. In 1969, at age forty-seven, Kerouac died from internal bleeding caused by cirrhosis of the liver.

Although known as the father of the Beat Generation, Kerouac never cared for this or any other label. His work consisted mostly of autobiographical novels and his style seemed spontaneous, though those who knew him understood that a great deal of thought went into each piece before he began writing. His use of language stems from the rhythm of breathing as it pertains to jazz music and to Buddhist meditation. This is evident in his most famous novel *On the Road*, which was an instant success.

Satori in Paris is Kerouac's account of ten days in Paris where he traces his family's name. However, the novel is about his interaction with the French, and his clashes with the culture, more than any genealogical search. Kerouac struggles with the language and writes as a lonesome traveler. (The Canadian French he knows so well does him little good in Paris.)

FROM CHAPTER ONE

Somewhere during my ten days in Paris (and Brittany) I received an illumination of some kind that seems to've changed me again, towards what I suppose'll be my pattern for another seven years or more: in effect, a *satori*: the Japanese word for "sudden illumination," "sudden awakening" or simply "kick in the eye." — Whatever, something *did* happen and in my first reveries after the trip and I'm back home regrouping all the confused rich events of those ten days, it seems the satori was handed to me by a taxi driver named Raymond Baillet, other times I think it might've been my paranoiac fear in the foggy streets of Brest Brittany at 3 A.M., other times I think it was Monsieur Casteljaloux and his dazzling beautiful secretary (a Bretonne with blue-black hair, green eyes, separated front teeth just right in eatable lips, white wool knit sweater, with gold bracelets and perfume) or the waiter who told me "*Paris est pourri*" (Paris is rotten) or the performance of Mozart's Requiem in old church of St. Germain des Prés with elated violinists swinging their elbows with joy because so many distinguished people had shown up crowding the pews and special chairs (and outside it's misting) or, in Heaven's name, *what*:

CHURCH OF SAINT-GERMAIN-DES-PRÉS

This is the oldest church in Paris originating in 542 when King Childebert built a basilica to house holy relics. Among the most famous tombs in this church are those of seventeenth-century philosopher René Descartes, poet Nicolas Boileau, and John Casimir, king of Poland, who became abbot of Saint-Germain-des-Prés in 1669.

The straight tree lanes of Tuileries Gardens? Or the roaring sway of the bridge over the booming holiday Seine which I crossed holding on to my hat knowing it was not the bridge (the makeshift one at Quai des Tuileries) but I myself swaying from too much cognac and nerves and no sleeping and jet airliner all the way from Florida twelve hours with airport anxieties, or bars, or anguishes, intervening?

As in an earlier, autobiographical book I'll use my real name here, full name in this case, Jean-Louis Lebris de Kérouac, because this story is about my search for this name in France, and I'm not afraid of giving the real name of Raymond Baillet to public scrutiny because all I have to say about him, in connection with the fact he may be the cause of my satori in Paris, is that he was polite, kind, efficient, hip, aloof and many other things and mainly just a cabdriver who happened to drive me to Orly airfield on my way back home from France: and sure he wont be in trouble because of that—And besides probably never will see his name in print because there are so many books being published these days in America and in France nobody has time to keep up with all of them, and if told by someone that his name appears in an American "novel" he'll probably never find out where to buy it in Paris, if it's ever translated at all, and if he does find it, it wont hurt him to read that he, Raymond Baillet, is a great gentleman and cabdriver who happened to impress an American during a fare ride to the airport.

Compris?

CHAPTER THIRTEEN

Paris is a place where you can really walk around at night and find what you dont want, O Pascal.

Trying to make my way to the Opera a hundred cars came charging around a blind curve-corner and like all the other pedestrians I waited to let them pass and then they all started across but I waited a few seconds looking the other charging cars over, all coming from six directions—Then I stepped off the curb and a car came around that curve all alone like the chaser running last in a Monaco race and right at me—I stepped back just in time—At the wheel a Frenchman completely convinced that no one else has a right to live or get to his mistress as fast as he does—As a New Yorker I run to dodge the free zipping roaring traffic of Paris but Parisians just stand and then stroll and leave it to the driver—And by God it works, I saw dozens of cars screech to a stop from 70 M.P.H. to let some stroller have his way!

I was going to the Opera also to eat in any restaurant that looked nice, it was one of my sober evenings dedicated to solitary studious walks, but O what grim rainy Gothic buildings and me walking well in the middle of those wide sidewalks so's to avoid dark doorways—What vistas of Nowhere City Night and hats and umbrellas—I couldn't even buy a newspaper—Thousands of people were coming out of some performance somewhere—I went to a crowded restaurant on Boulevard des Italiens and sat way at the end of the bar by myself on a high stool and watched, wet and helpless, as waiters mashed up raw hamburg with Worcestershire sauce and other things and other waiters rushed by holding up steaming trays of good food—The one sympathetic counterman brought menu and Alsatian beer I ordered and I told him to wait awhile—He didn't understand that, drinking without eating at once, because he is partner to the secret of charming French eaters:—they rush at the very beginning with *hors d'oeuvres and bread,* and then plunge into their entrees (this is practically always before even a slug of wine) and then they slow down and start lingering, now the wine to wash the mouth, now comes the *talk,* and now the second half of the meal, wine, dessert and coffee, something I cannae do.

BOULEVARD DES ITALIENS

Named for an Italian theater that was built in 1783, soon after the Revolution, this is one of the four main boulevards in Paris. Before the First World War this area enjoyed stylish shops and restaurants like Café de Paris and du café Tortoni. The Italian theater is now gone and the Opera-Comique has taken its place. The chic cafés and shops have been largely replaced with financial institutions.

In any case I'm drinking my second beer and reading the menu and notice an American guy is sitting five stools away but he is so mean looking in his absolute disgust with Paris I'm afraid to say "Hey, you American?"—He's come to Paris expecting he woulda wound up under a cherry tree in blossom in the sun with pretty girls on his lap and people dancing around him, instead he's been wandering the rainy streets alone in all that jargon, doesnt even know where the whore district is, or Notre Dame, or some small cafe they told him about back in Glennon's bar on Third Avenue, *nothing*—When he pays for his sandwich he literally throws the money on the counter "You wouldnt help me figure what the real price is anyway, and besides shove it up your you-know-what I'm going back to my old mine nets in Norfolk and get drunk with Bill Eversole in the bookie joint and all the other things you dumb frogs dont know about," and stalks out in poor misunderstood raincoat and disillusioned rubbers—

Then in come two American schoolteachers of Iowa, sisters on a big trip to Paris, they've apparently got a hotel room round the corner and aint left it except to ride the sightseeing buses which pick em up at the door, but they know this nearest restaurant and have just come down to buy a couple of oranges for tomorrow morning because the only oranges in France are apparently Valencias imported from Spain and too expensive for anything so avid as quick simple *break of fast*. So to my amazement I hear the first clear bell tones of American speech in a week:—"You got some oranges here?"

"*Pardon?*"—the counterman.

"There they are in that glass case," says the other gal.

"Okay—see?" pointing, "two oranges," and showing two fingers, and the counterman takes out the two oranges and puts em in a bag and says crisply thru his throat with those Arabic Parisian "r's":—

"*Trois francs cinquante.*" In other words, 35¢ an orange but the old gals dont care what it costs and besides they dont understand what he's said.

"What's *that* mean?"

"*Pardon?*"

"Alright, I'll hold out my palm and take your kwok-kowk-kwark out of it, all we want's the oranges" and the two ladies burst into peals of screaming laughter like on the porch and the cat politely removes three francs fifty centimes from her hand, leaving the change, and they walk out lucky they're not alone like that American guy—

I ask my counterman what's real good and he says Alsatian Choucroute which he brings—It's just hotdogs, potatos and sauerkraut, but such hotdogs as chew like butter and have a flavor delicate as the scent of wine, butter and garlic all cooking together and floating out a cafe kitchen door—The sauerkraut no better'n

Pennsylvania, potatos we got from Maine and San Jose, but O yes I forgot:—with it all, on top, is a weird soft strip of bacon which is really like ham and is the best bite of all.

I had come to France to do nothing but walk and eat and this was my first meal and my last, ten days.

But in referring back to what I said to Pascal, as I was leaving this restaurant (paid 24 francs, or almost $5 for this simple platter) I heard a howling in the rainy boulevard—A maniacal Algerian had gone mad and was shouting at everyone and everything and was holding something I couldnt see, very small knife or object or pointed ring or something—I had to stop in the door— People hurried by scared—I didn't want to be *seen* by him hurrying away—The waiters came out and watched with me—He approached us stabbing outdoor wicker chairs as he came—The headwaiter and I looked calmly into each other's eyes as tho to say "Are we together?"—But my counterman began talking to the mad Arab, who was actually light haired and probably half French half Algerian, and it became some sort of conversation and I walked around and went home in a now-driving rain, had to hail a cab.

Romantic raincoats.

100 — PARIS. Le Palais-Royal. ND Phot

Palais Royal

The Razor's Edge

BY W. SOMERSET MAUGHAM (1944)

W. Somerset Maugham was born in Paris in 1874 to English parents. His father managed legal affairs at the British Embassy in Paris. Maugham attended the King's School but felt stifled and at sixteen refused to go back. His uncle provided an opportunity for him to study literature and philosophy at Heidelberg University in Germany. He went on to study medicine, but eventually gave his full attention to writing. During World War II, Maugham lived in the United States. After the war he returned to England, then in 1946 he returned to France where he remained until his death in 1965.

Maugham enjoyed talking about his own development as a writer. He is known for saying that there should be no rules in writing. In his earlier works he tried to force a style of writing and voice that was not his own. Maugham flourished as a writer once he stripped away all ideas of what made for good writing and simply trusted his own voice and wrote. He strove for an economical style much like that of Maupassant, but compared to the great French author, Maugham's skills were limited. In *The Summing Up* (1938), he speaks of this failure, stating that he stood "in the first row of the second-raters." His cynical undertone and intriguing characters made him a favorite among readers then and now, despite what he and his critics said. Maugham enjoyed huge financial success and popularity as a writer during his lifetime.

Of Human Bondage is considered his masterpiece, and is largely autobiographical. *The Razor's Edge* was his last major work and among his most reflective and enjoyable stories to read. The novel is set in Paris after World War I. Larry, a young man from Chicago, turns down a promising career in banking and lives hand-to-mouth in Paris between trips to other countries in search of the meaning of life.

FROM PART FOUR, CHAPTER THREE

In all big cities there are self-contained groups that exist without inter communication, small worlds within a greater world that lead their lives, their members dependent upon one another for companionship, as though they inhabited islands separated from each other by an unnavigable strait. Of no city, in my experience, is this more true than of Paris. There high society seldom admits outsiders into its midst, the politicians live in their own corrupt circle, bourgeoisie, great and small, frequent one another, writers congregate with writers (it is remarkable in André Gide's *Journal* to see with how few people he seems to have been intimate who did not follow his own calling), painters hobnob with painters, and musicians with musicians. The same thing is true of London, but in a less marked degree; there birds of a feather flock much less together, and there are a dozen houses where at the same table you may meet a duchess, an actress, a painter, a member of parliament, a lawyer, a dressmaker, and an author.

AVENUE FOCH

Avenue Foch was originally called Avenue du Bois de Boulogne since it ran along the edge of the Bois de Boulogne city park. In 1929 the street was renamed to honor Ferdinand Foch, a French soldier known for his brilliance. The Avenue is the widest in Paris and lined from end to end with chestnut trees.

The events of my life have led me to one time and another to dwell transitory in pretty well all the worlds of Paris, even (through Elliott) in the closed world of the Boulevard St. Germain; but that which I liked best, better than the discreet circle that has its center in what is now called the Avenue Foch, better than the cosmopolitan crew that patronize Larue's and the Café de Paris, better than the noisy sordid gaiety of Montmartre, is that section of which the artery is the Boulevard du Montparnasse.

MONTMARTRE

During Roman times Montmartre was a small vineyard town at the top of a hill, but the area was engulfed by Paris's expansion in the nineteenth century and Montmartre quickly became a favorite location for artists to both work and live. Between the two world wars the area became more expensive, forcing artists like Picasso and Maurice Utrillo to look toward Montparnasse as a more affordable place to dwell. Today, the area has a steady stream of tourists in search of paintings and plenty of street painters to provide them.

In my youth I spent a year in a tiny apartment near the Lion de Belfort, on the fifth floor, from which I had a spacious view of the cemetery.

LION DE BELFORT

The original Lion de Belfort, created by Frederic Bartholdi, who also created the Statue of Liberty in New York, is a domineering presence in the small town of Belfort, France. Place Denfert-Rochereau in Paris and Jardin Botanique de Montréal have the only two copies of the sculpture. The Lion was made in honor of the fight of seventeen thousand men, led by Colonel Denfert-Rochereau, against forty thousand Prussian soldiers.

Montparnasse has still for me the tranquil air of a provincial town that was characteristic of it then. When I pass through the dingy narrow Rue d'Odessa I remember with a pang the shabby restaurant where we used to foregather to dine, painters and illustrators and sculptors, I, but for Arnold Bennett on occasion, the only writer, and sit late discussing excitedly, absurdly, angrily, painting and literature. It is still a pleasure to me to stroll down the boulevard and look at the young people who are as young as I was then and invent stories for myself about them. When I have nothing better to do I take a taxi and go and sit in the old Café du Dôme.

CAFÉ DU DÔME

Upon its opening in 1898, intellectuals, writers, and artists gathered at the Café Du Dôme. It was the first of its kind in Montparnasse and was often referred to as the "Anglo-American café." In the early 1900s, a patron could get a hot meal for a low price, so it was popular among up-and-coming writers and artists. Today, it is a seafood restaurant, but hardly a place where a poor artist might afford a good meal.

It is no longer what it was then, the meeting place exclusively of Bohemia; the small tradesmen of the neighborhood have taken to visiting it, and strangers from the other side of the Seine come to it in the hope of seeing a world that has ceased to exist. Students come to it still, of course, painters and writers, but most of them are foreigners; and when you sit there you hear around you as much Russian, Spanish, German, and English as French. But I have a notion that they are saying very much the same sort of things as we said forty years ago, only they speak of Picasso instead of Manet and of Andre Breton instead of Guillaume Apollinaire. My heart goes out to them.

FROM PART SIX, CHAPTER THREE

One evening I went to the Théâtre Français to see *Bérénice*. I had read it of course, but had never seen it played, and since it is seldom given I was unwilling to miss the opportunity. It is not one of Racine's best plays, for the subject is too tenuous to support five acts, but it is moving and contains passages that are justly famous.

THE THÉÂTRE FRANÇAIS

The Théâtre Français, built between 1786 and 1790, is the oldest national theater in France. It is also the home of the Comédie Française, founded in 1680 by Louis XIV. The director of the troupe has been appointed by the government since 1812 when Napoleon made it a state company. The Comédie Française primarily performs classical French repertoire, including Corneille and Racine along with some modern classics of Paul Claudel and Samuel Beckett.

The story is founded on a brief passage in Tacitus: Titus, who loved the Queen of Palestine, with passion and who had even, as was supposed, promised her marriage, for reasons of state sent her away from Rome during the first days of his reign in despite of his desires and in despite of hers. For the Senate and the people of Rome were violently opposed to their Emperor's alliance with a foreign queen. The play is concerned with the struggle in his breast between love and duty, and when he falters, it is Bérénice who in the end, assured that he loves her, confirms his purpose and separates herself from him forever.

I suppose only a Frenchman can appreciate to the full the grace and grandeur of Racine and the music of his verse, but even a foreigner, once he has accustomed himself to the periwigged formality of the style, can hardly fail to be moved by his passionate tenderness and by the nobility of his sentiment. Racine knew as few have done how much drama is contained in the human voice. To me at all events the roll of those mellifluous Alexandrines is a sufficient substitute for action, and I find the long speeches, worked up with infinite skill to the expected climax, every bit as thrilling as any hair-raising adventure of the movies.

There was an interval after the third act and I went out to smoke a cigarette in the foyer over which presides Houdon's Voltaire with his toothless, sardonic grin. Someone touched me on the shoulder, I turned around, perhaps with a slight movement of annoyance, for I wanted to be left with the exaltation with which those sonorous lines had filled me, and saw Larry. As always, I was glad to see him. It was a year since I had set eyes on him, and I suggested that at the end of the play we should meet and have a glass of beer together. Larry said he was hungry, for he had had no dinner, and proposed that we should go to Montmartre. We found one another in due course and stepped out into the open. The Théâtre Français has a musty fug that is peculiar to it. It is impregnated with the body odor of those unnumbered generations of sour-faced, unwashed women called ouvreuses who show you to your seat and domineeringly await their tip. It was a relief to get into the fresh air, and since the night was fine we walked. The arc lamps in the Avenue de l'Opéra glared so defiantly that the stars above, as though too proud to compete, shrouded their brightness in the dark of their infinite distance. As we walked we spoke of the performance we had just seen. Larry was disappointed. He would have liked it to be more natural, the lines spoken as people naturally speak and the gestures less theatrical. I thought his point of view mistaken. It was rhetoric, magnificent rhetoric, and I had a notion that it should be spoken rhetorically. I liked the regular thump of the rhymes; and the stylized gestures, handed down in a long tradition, seemed to me to suit the temper of that formal act. I could not but think that that was how Racine would have wished his play to be played. I had admired the way in which the actors had contrived to be human, passionate, and true within the limitations that confined them. Art is triumphant when it can use convention as an instrument of its own purpose.

We reached the Avenue de Clichy and went into the Brasserie Graf. It was not long past midnight and the room was crowded, but we found a table and ordered ourselves eggs and bacon.

Champs Elysees, 1921

A Woman's Life

BY GUY DE MAUPASSANT (1883)

Born in Château de Miromesniel, Dieppe, in 1850, Guy De Maupassant spent his childhood in Normandy. When he was eleven his parents separated and his mother settled in the coastal town of Érretat. He served in the army during the Franco-Prussian War and from 1872 to 1880 he worked at the Ministry of Education. He published his first poem, "Des Vers," in 1880 and in the same year he also published an anthology titled *Les Soirées de Médan*. He proved to be a prolific author, writing six novels, three travel books, and an estimated three hundred stories. He enjoyed tremendous success as a writer but suffered from bouts of severe mental illness. Themes of mental suffering run throughout his works. He committed suicide in 1892. He was considered one of France's greatest writers both in his lifetime and even still long after his death.

Like his mentor and friend, Gustave Flaubert, Maupassant's writing style was controlled and economical. His narrative is mostly objective and he wrote about everyday life and events that brought new emotions and actions.

Maupassant's first novel, *Une Vie (A Woman's Life)*, originally published in 1883 and translated into the following English version in 1909, is set in the late 1800s largely in rural France at a time when Paris was growing more sophisticated and industrious. The novel goes through the stages of one woman's life, Jeanne, from her hopeful youth to her later years when it seems that her son and the world have outgrown any use for her. In this section, Jeanne, now old, feels abandoned by her son. Upon learning that he is engaged, she decides to go to Paris and find him. She has not been to Paris in over twenty years and the city has changed in ways she could never have imagined.

FROM CHAPTER THIRTEEN

Another spring and summer passed away, and when the autumn came again with its rainy days, its dull, gray skies, its heavy clouds, Jeanne felt so weary of the life she was leading that she determined to make a supreme attempt to regain possession of her Poulet. Surely the young man's passion must have cooled by this time, and she wrote him a touching, pitiful letter:

"My Dear Child—I am coming to entreat you to return to me. Think how I am left, lonely, aged and ill, the whole year with only a servant. I am living now in a little house by the roadside and it is very miserable for me, but if you were here everything would seem different. You are all I have in the world, and I have not seen you for seven years. You will never know how unhappy I have been and how my every thought was centered in you. You were my life, my soul, my only hope, my only love, and you are away from me, you have forsaken me.

"Oh! come back, my darling Poulet, come back, and let me hold you in my arms again; come back to your old mother who so longs to see you.

"Jeanne."

A few days later came the following reply:

"My Dear Mother—I should only be too glad to come and see you, but I have not a penny; send me some money and I will come. I had myself been thinking of coming to speak to you about a plan which, if carried out, would permit me to do as you desire.

"I shall never be able to repay the disinterested affection of the woman who has shared all my troubles, but I can at least make a public recognition of her faithful love and devotion. Her behavior is all you could desire; she is well-educated and well-read and you cannot imagine what a comfort she has been to me. I should be a brute if I did not make her some recompense, and I ask your permission to marry her. Then we could all live together in your new house, and you would forgive my follies. I am convinced that you would give your consent at once, if you knew her; I assure you she is very lady-like and quiet, and I know you would like her. As for me, I could not live without her.

"I shall await your reply with every impatience, dear mother. We both send you much love.—Your son,

"Vicomte Paul de Lamare."

Jeanne was thunderstruck. As she sat with the letter on her knees, she could see so plainly through the designs of this woman who had not once let Paul return to his friends, but had always kept him at her side while she patiently waited until his mother should give in and consent to anything and everything in the irresistible desire of having her son with her again; and it was with bitter pain that she thought of how Paul obstinately persisted in preferring this creature to herself. "He does not love me, he does not love me," she murmured over and over again.

"He wants to marry her now," she said, when Rosalie came in. The servant stared. "Oh! madame, you surely will not consent to it. M. Paul can't bring that hussy here."

All the pride in Jeanne's nature rose in revolt at the thought, and though she was bowed down with grief, she replied decidedly:

"No, Rosalie, never. But since he won't come here I will go to him, and we will see which of us two will have the greater influence over him."

She wrote to Paul at once, telling him that she was coming to Paris, and would see him anywhere but at the house where he was living with that wretch. Then while she awaited his reply, she began to make all her preparations for the journey, and Rosalie commenced to pack her mistress's linen and clothes in an old trunk.

"You haven't a single thing to put on," exclaimed the servant, as she was folding up an old, badly-made dress. "I won't have you go with such clothes; you'd be a disgrace to everyone, and the Paris ladies would think you were a servant."

Jeanne let her have her own way, and they both went to Goderville and chose some green, checked stuff, which they left with the dressmaker to be made up. Then they went to see Me. Roussel the lawyer, who went to Paris for a fortnight every year, to obtain a few directions, for it was twenty-eight years since Jeanne had been to the capital. He gave them a great deal of advice about crossing the roads and the way to avoid being robbed, saying that the safest plan was to carry only just as much money as was necessary in the pockets and to sew the rest in the lining of the dress; then he talked for a long time about the restaurants where the charges were moderate, and mentioned two or three to which ladies could go, and he recommended Jeanne to stay at the Hôtel de Normandie, which was near the railway station.

HOTEL NORMANDIE

The Hotel Normandie is still in business, and still priced for travelers with a modest budget. The rooms are small, the accommodations are minimal, but the location, at Four Rue D'amsterdam in the ninth Arrondissement, is nice.

He always stayed there himself, and she could say he had sent her. There had been a railway between Paris and Havre for the last six years, but Jeanne had never seen one of these steam-engines of which everyone was talking, and which were revolutionizing the whole country.

The day passed on, but still there came no answer from Paul. Every morning, for a fortnight, Jeanne had gone along the road to meet the postman, and had asked, in a voice which she could not keep steady: "You have nothing for me to-day, Père Malandain?" And the answer was always the same: "No nothing yet, ma bonne dame."

Fully persuaded that it was that woman who was preventing Paul from answering, Jeanne determined not to wait any longer, but to start at once. She wanted to take Rosalie with her, but the maid would not go because of increasing the expense of the journey, and she only allowed her mistress to take three hundred francs with her.

"If you want any more money," she said, "write to me, and I'll tell the lawyer to forward you some; but if I give you any more now, Monsieur Paul will have it all."

Then one December morning, Denis Lecoq's gig came to take them both to the railway station, for Rosalie was going to accompany her mistress as far as that. When they reached the station, they found out first how much the tickets were, then, when the trunk had been labeled and the ticket bought, they stood watching the rails, both too much occupied in wondering what the train would be like to think of the sad cause of this journey. At last a distant whistle made them look round, and they saw a large, black machine approaching, which came up with a terrible noise, dragging after it a long chain of little rolling houses. A porter opened the door of one of these little huts, and Jeanne kissed Rosalie and got in.

"Au revoir, madame. I hope you will have a pleasant journey, and will soon be back again."

"Au revoir, Rosalie."

There was another whistle, and the string of carriages moved slowly off, gradually going faster and faster, till they reached a terrific speed. In Jeanne's compartment there were only two other passengers, who were both asleep, and she sat and watched the fields and farms and villages rush past. She was frightened at the speed at which she was going, and the feeling came over her that she was entering a new phase of life, and was being hurried towards a very different world from that in which she had spent her peaceful girlhood and her monotonous life.

It was evening when she reached Paris. A porter took her trunk, and she followed closely at his heels, sometimes almost running for fear of losing sight of him, and feeling frightened as she was pushed about by the swaying crowd through which she did not know how to pass.

"I was recommended here by Me. Roussel," she hastened to say when she was in the hôtel office.

The landlady, a big, stolid-looking woman, was sitting at the desk.

"Who is Me. Roussel?" she asked.

"The lawyer from Goderville, who stays here every year," replied Jeanne, in surprise.

"Very likely he does," responded the big woman, "but I don't know him. Do you want a room?"

"Yes, madame."

A waiter shouldered the luggage and led the way upstairs.

Jeanne followed, feeling very low-spirited and depressed, and sitting down at a little table, she ordered some soup and the wing of a chicken to be sent up to her, for she had had nothing to eat since day-break. She thought of how she had passed through this same town on her return from her wedding tour, as she ate her supper by the miserable light of one candle, and of how Julien had then first shown himself in his true character. But then she was young and brave and hopeful; now she felt old and timid; and the least thing worried and frightened her.

When she had finished her supper, she went to the window and watched the crowded street. She would have liked to go out if she had dared, but she thought she should be sure to lose herself, so she went to bed. But she had hardly yet got over the bustle of the journey, and that, and the noise and the sensation of being in a strange place, kept her awake. The hours passed on, and the noises outside gradually ceased, but still she could not sleep, for she was accustomed to the sound, peaceful sleep of the country, which is so different from the semi-repose of a great city. Here she was conscious of a sort of restlessness all around her; the murmur of voices reached her ears, and every now and then a board creaked, a door shut, or a bell rang. She was just dozing off, about two o'clock in the morning, when a woman suddenly began to scream in a neighboring room. Jeanne started up in bed, and next she thought she heard a man laughing. As dawn approached she became more and more anxious to see Paul, and as soon as it was light, she got up and dressed.

He lived in the Rue du Sauvage, and she meant to follow Rosalie's advice about spending as little as possible, and walk there. It was a fine day, though the wind was keen, and there were a great many people hurrying along the pavements. Jeanne walked along the street as quickly as she could. When she reached the other end, she was to turn to the right, then to the left; then she would come to a square, where she was to ask again. She could not find the square, and a baker from whom she inquired the way gave her different directions altogether. She started on again, missed the way, wandered about, and in trying to follow other directions, lost herself entirely. She walked on and on, and was just going to hail a cab when she saw the Seine. Then she decided to walk along the quays, and in about an hour she reached the dark, dirty lane called Rue du Sauvage.

When she came to the number she was seeking, she was so excited that she stood before the door unable to move another step. Poulet was there, in that house! Her hands and knees trembled violently, and it was some moments before she could enter and walk along the passage to the doorkeeper's box.

"Will you go and tell M. Paul de Lamare that an old lady friend of his mother's, is waiting to see him?" she said, slipping a piece of money into the man's hand.

"He does not live here now, madame," answered the doorkeeper.

She started.

"Ah! Where—where is he living now?" she gasped.

"I do not know."

She felt stunned, and it was some time before she could speak again.

"When did he leave?" she asked at last, controlling herself by a violent effort.

The man was quite ready to tell her all he knew.

"About a fortnight ago," he replied. "They just walked out of the house one evening and didn't come back. They owed all over the neighborhood, so you may guess they didn't leave any address."

Tongues of flame were dancing before Jeanne's eyes, as if a gun were being fired off close to her face; but she wanted to find Poulet, and that kept her up and made her stand opposite the doorkeeper, as if she were calmly thinking.

"Then he did not say anything when he left?"

"No, nothing at all; they went away to get out of paying their debts."

"But he will have to send for his letters."

"He'll send a good many times before he gets them, then; besides, they didn't have ten in a twelvemonth, though I took them up one two days before they left."

That must have been the one she sent.

"Listen," she said, hastily. "I am his mother, and I have come to look for him. Here are ten francs for yourself. If you hear anything from or about him, let me know at once at the Hôtel de Normandie, Rue du Havre, and you shall be well paid for your trouble."

RUE DE HAVRE

This street runs between rue Saint-Lazare and Boulevard Haussmann but is best known for running along the front of the Gare Saint-Lazare—one of the main destinations for Paris Métro travelers from Havre-Caumartin. Its proximity to a train station still keeps la rue lined with hotels, and reason to be in novels both past and present.

"You may depend upon me, madame," answered the door-keeper; and Jeanne went away.

She hastened along the streets as if she were bent on an important mission, but she was not looking or caring whither she was going. She walked close to the walls, pushed and buffeted by errand boys and porters; crossed the roads, regardless of the vehicles and the shouts of the drivers; stumbled against the curbstones, which she did not see; and hurried on and on, unconscious of everything and everyone. At last she found herself in some gardens, and, feeling too weary to walk any further, she dropped on a seat. She sat there a long while, apparently unaware that the tears were running down her cheeks, and that passersby stopped to look at her. At last the bitter cold made her rise to go, but her legs would hardly carry her, so weak and exhausted was she. She would have liked some soup, but she dared not go into a restaurant, for she knew people could see she was in trouble, and it made her feel timid and ashamed. When she passed an eating-place she would stop a moment at the door, look inside, and see all the people sitting at the tables eating, and then go on again, saying to herself: "I will go into the next one"; but when she came to the next her courage always failed her again. In the end she went into a baker's shop, and bought a little crescent-shaped roll, which she ate as she went along. She was very thirsty, but she did not know where to go to get anything to drink, so she went without.

She passed under an arch, and found herself in some more gardens with arcades running all round them, and she recognized the Palais Royal.

PALAIS ROYAL

The Palais Royal was built in 1624 for Cardinal Richelieu. He died in 1642 and left the palace to the French crown. Since then it has endured a history filled with royal drama. From 1780 to 1837 it was the center of Parisian political and social intrigue. Between 1871 and 1874, Louis-Philippe d'Orléans, cousin of King Louis XVI, expanded the palace by adding shops. For some time the palace even allowed gambling.

Her walk in the sun had made her warm again, so she sat down for another hour or two. A crowd of people flowed into the gardens—an elegant crowd composed of beautiful women and wealthy men, who only lived for dress and pleasure, and who chatted and smiled and bowed as they sauntered along. Feeling ill at ease amidst this brilliant throng, Jeanne rose to go away; but suddenly the thought struck her that perhaps she might meet Paul here, and she began to walk from end to end of the gardens, with hasty, furtive steps, carefully scanning every face she met.

Soon she saw that people turned to look and laugh at her, and she hurried away, thinking it was her odd appearance and her green-checked dress, which Rosalie had chosen and had made up, that attracted everyone's attention and smiles. She hardly dared ask her way, but she did at last venture, and when she had reached her hotel, she passed the rest of the day sitting on a chair at the foot of the bed. In the evening she dined off some soup and a little meat, like the day before, and then undressed and went to bed, performing all the duties of her toilet quite mechanically, from sheer habit.

The next morning she went to the police office to see if she could get any help there towards the discovery of her son's whereabouts. They told her they could not promise her anything, but that they would attend to the matter. After she had left the police office, she wandered about the streets, in the hopes of meeting her child, and she felt more friendless and forsaken among the busy crowds than she did in the midst of the lovely fields.

When she returned to the hotel in the evening, she was told that a man from M. Paul had asked for her, and was coming again the next day. All the blood in her body seemed to suddenly rush to her heart and she could not close her eyes all night. Perhaps it was Paul himself? Yes, it must be so, although his appearance did not tally with the description the hotel people had given of the man who had called, and, when, about nine o'clock in the morning, there came a knock at her door, she cried, "Come in!" expecting her son to rush into her arms held open to receive him.

But it was a stranger who entered—a stranger who began to apologize for disturbing her and to explain that he had come about some money Paul owed him. As he spoke she felt herself beginning to cry, and she tried to hide her tears from the man by wiping them away with the end of her finger as soon as they reached the corners of her eyes. The man had heard of her arrival from the concierge at the Rue du Sauvage, and as he could not find Paul he had come to his mother. He held out a paper which Jeanne mechanically took; she saw "90 francs" written on it, and she drew out the money and paid the man. She did not go out at all that day, and the next morning more creditors appeared. She gave them all the money she had left, except twenty francs, and wrote and told Rosalie how she was placed.

Until her servant's answer came she passed the days in wandering aimlessly about the streets. She did not know what to do or how to kill the long, miserable hours; there was no one who knew of her troubles, or to whom she could go for sympathy, and her one desire was to get away from this city and to return to her little house beside the lonely road, where, a few days before, she had felt she could not bear to live because it was so dull and lonely. Now she was sure she could live nowhere else but in that little home where all her mournful habits had taken root.

At last, one evening, she found a letter from Rosalie awaiting her with two hundred francs enclosed. "Come back as soon as possible, Madame Jeanne," wrote the maid, "for I shall send you nothing more. As for M. Paul, I will go and fetch him myself the next time we hear anything from him.—With best respects, your servant, Rosalie."

And Jeanne starred back to Batteville one bitterly cold, snowy morning.

Chasing Cézanne

BY PETER MAYLE (1997)

Born in 1939 in Brighton, England, Peter Mayle is a British author who spent fifteen years in advertising before changing careers. In 1975 he began writing educational books and published his first book, *Will I Go to Heaven*, in 1978. Seven books later, in 1990, with the publication of *A Year in Provence*, Mayle became an international bestselling author. Since then he has written several more books on life in Provence, along with books about excursions throughout France. He has written over twenty books and

Pendant la Belle Saison, 1906

contributes to *The Sunday Times*, *The Financial Times*, *The Independent*, *GQ*, and *Esquire*. In 2002, he was awarded the rank of Chevalier de la Légion d'Honneur (Knight of the French Legion of Honor). Today, he and his wife live in Provence.

Mayle's writing is light-hearted, charming, and always told through a most likable narrator. His stories are fast-paced, energetic, and, at times, satirical. He writes about the places his characters are in and the food they are eating with far greater detail than he does about the characters themselves. In a Mayle novel, few things matter more than the description of a fine dinner and the view from the table where his characters are dining.

Chasing Cézanne is a mystery travelogue set in the art world, travels through Paris, Provence, and New York. Freelance photographer Andre Kelly visits the home of the wealthy Denoyer family in the south of France to take photos for a decorating magazine. When he gets there he learns that the family is away, but he sees someone loading the family's *Cézanne* into a plumbing van. Stunned, he takes a photo and soon thereafter a whirlwind investigation begins. Cyrus, an art dealer, is brought into the fold to help solve the mystery. Eventually, the investigation takes them to Paris. While Andre Kelly enjoys a hotel he knows well and Lucy, Andre's girlfriend, visits the city for the first time, Cyrus makes some interesting discoveries in the investigation.

FROM CHAPTER FIFTEEN

They were staying at the Montalembert, in a small side street off the Rue du Bac, *vieux Paris* on the outside, cool and contemporary within, a hotel much in favor among the black-uniformed ornaments of the fashion world.

THE MONTALEMBERT

Located in the Latin Quarter, the Montalembert is an exquisite boutique hotel that sits near the Saint-Germain-des-Prés district. Even with their outstanding breakfast, fine service, and impeccable décor, this luxury hotel's location is still its most breathtaking feature. Art galleries, shops, and the best cafés in Paris are all within close walking distance.

Andre had chosen it not simply for its looks and its location but because the staff were charming, young, and—flying in the face of Parisian convention—genuinely friendly. There was also the bar.

The bar at the Montalembert, just to the left of the lobby, is a place where one could easily spend an entire day. Breakfast, lunch, and dinner are served there. Drinks flow from late morning onward. The world comes and goes, deals are done, love affairs begin (seldom ended, for some reason; perhaps the lighting is too cheerful for tears and remorse). There are no TV sets. The entertainment is human.

As they were waiting to check in, Lucy cast an appraising eye over two wafer-thin, high-gloss women sitting with glasses of champagne, puffing cigarettes and recoiling after each puff, with a twist of long and elegant necks, from the smoke. "Babes," said Lucy. "Look at them. They're comparing cheekbones."

Cyrus patted her shoulder. "Two suburban housewives, my dear. Probably discussing what to give their husbands for dinner."

Lucy pursed her lips, trying to imagine either of them anywhere near a kitchen. Andre turned away from the front desk, two keys in his hand. "Lulu, stop staring at those nice old ladies."

He gave one of the keys to Cyrus and shepherded them into an elevator of that particular Gallic size which encourages close personal relationships. If the occupants are strangers at the beginning of the ride, they certainly aren't by the end.

Lucy investigated their room with the thoroughness of a Michelin inspector, running her fingers over the rosewood, testing the bed in its crisp navy and white striped cover, admiring the steel and slate of the bathroom, throwing open the tall casement windows that overlooked a tumble of Parisian rooftops, rooftops like no others in the world. Andre smiled as he watched her dart from one discovery to the next.

"Well?" he said. "Will it do?"

"I can't believe I'm here." She took his hand and pulled him over to the window. "Look," she said, *"Paris!"*

"So it is," he said. "What do you want to see first?"

"Everything."

* * *

There are several thousand starting points for such an ambitious enterprise in Paris, but few more pleasant or fascinating for the first-time visitor than Deux Magots, the quintessential café on the Boulevard Saint-Germain. Its critics may say that there are too many tourists; that the waiters, world-weary and flat of foot, have made an art form of curmudgeonly service; that the prices are inhospitably severe. Much of this may be true, but there is nowhere quite like a table on the terrace for watching Parisians do what Parisians do so well; strolling, posing, inspecting each other's spring outfits, exchanging multiple shrugs, pouts and kisses, seeing and being seen.

As morning gave way to noon, it had become mild and sunny, with a light breeze off the Seine, the best kind of street weather. The leaves on the trees, not yet made dull by gasoline fumes, shone against their branches as though they had been freshly painted a clean, strong green. It was the kind of day that had turned April in Paris into a song.

Lucy sat between the two men, enthralled. She could have been watching tennis, her head swiveling from side to side, not wanting to miss anything. How unlike New York it all was. There were so many smokers, so many dogs, so many old and beautiful buildings, a feeling of spaciousness that was impossible in a sky-scraper city. The coffee was stronger, the air tasted different, even Andre was different. She watched him with the waiter. When he spoke French, his body changed gear and became more fluid, his hands and shoulders constantly on the move, his jaw and bottom lip thrust forward as he pronounced those words that sounded so exotic to ears accustomed to the harsher cadences of Anglo-Saxon speech. So fast, too. Everybody spoke so fast.

Cyrus suggested that they eat lightly, saving themselves for what was likely to be a long and elaborate dinner, and after cof-fee they ordered glasses of Beaujolais and ham sandwiches, sub-stantial half-baguettes, Lucy's first taste of true French bread and Normandy butter. She took a first appreciative bite, then stopped eating to look at Andre.

"Why isn't everyone in Paris fat?" she said, waving a hand at the people around them. "Look at the stuff they're putting away and the wine. And then they're going to do it all over again at din-ner. How do they do it? Do they have some special diet?"

"Absolutely," said Andre. "No more than three courses at lunch, no more than five courses at dinner, and they never drink before breakfast. Isn't that right, Cyrus?"

"Something like that, dear boy. Don't forget the daily bottle of wine and a small cognac at bedtime—oh, and plenty of butter in the cooking. Very little exercise, too. That's important. And a pack of cigarettes a day."

Lucy shook her head. "OK, maybe it was a silly question. But so far, I haven't seen a single fat person. Not one."

"It's part of what they call the French Paradox," Andre said. "Do you remember? There was a big fuss about it a few years ago. I think it all started when they did a survey of twenty countries and their eating habits. They were looking at the relationship between national diets and the incidence of heart disease."

Cyrus looked thoughtfully at his wine. "I'm not sure I want to hear about this."

Andre grinned. "You'll be fine as long as you stay here. When the results came out, they showed that the country with the healthiest diet was Japan—not surprising, really, when you think that they mainly eat fish and rice. But the big surprise was the runner-up. Number two out of twenty countries was France; despite the bread, the cheese, the foie gras, the sauces, the three-hour lunches, the alcohol. So of course, people wanted to know why. They thought there must be a secret, some kind of diet trick that allowed you to eat what you wanted and get away with it. And what they came up with as the explanation was red wine."

Cyrus nodded. "I remember now," he said. "It was on television, wasn't it? Most of the liquor stores in America sold out of Cabernet Sauvignon in forty-eight hours."

"That's right. Then someone started talking about the incidence of cirrhosis of the liver in France being higher than in the States, and everyone went back to hamburgers and Coke."

"Where did America come on the list?" Lucy asked.

"Oh, way down. Something like fourteen or fifteen, I think. Red wine isn't going to change that. Actually, my theory is that red wine has less to do with it than people think. Obviously, what you eat and drink is important, but so is *how* you eat and drink. And there's an enormous difference in national habits. Food for most Americans is fuel—eat in the car, eat on the street, finish dinner in fifteen minutes. Food for the French is treated as a pleasure. They take their time over it. They concentrate on it. They like being at the table, and they don't eat between meals. You'll never catch the President of France sucking up potato chips at his desk. Cooking is respected here. It's accepted as an art. The top chefs are almost like movie stars." Andre paused and finished his wine. "Sorry. That sounded like a lecture. But it's true." He turned to Lucy. "Wait till you see the food tonight."

"I didn't tell you," said Cyrus. "I called Franzen from the hotel."

"Is everything OK?"

Cyrus rolled his eyes. "He's an enthusiast. Couldn't stop talking about the menu—apparently Senderens is one of the great chefs, and Franzen sounded as though he already had his knife and fork out. We're meeting him there at eight. He seemed very friendly, I must say, told me to call him Nico. I have a feeling we're going to get on."

Lucy was watching a tall blonde in black leather stride through the boulevard traffic with a borzoi, ignoring the cars, both girl and dog walking with haughty, head-high grace. The effect was marred by the dog's decision to cock his leg against the rear wheel of a parked motorcycle while the owner was attempting to get on. The owner expostulated, his leg also cocked across the saddle. The girl ignored him and strode on.

Lucy shook her head. "In New York, they'd be in a fight by now. Then the dog would be sued." She shook her head again and turned to Cyrus. "Can we talk business?"

"Of course."

"Do you think I should wear black tonight? No, I'm kidding. What do you hope to get out of Franzen?"

"Well, let's see." Cyrus straightened his bow tie, his eyes looking across the boulevard at the Brasserie Lipp.

THE BRASSERIE ON BOULEVARD ST. GERMAIN

The Brasserie Lipp prefers to be called a brasserie, rather than a restaurant, since it considers itself a place to drink beer, wine, and coffee. The fact that the food, Alsatian cuisine, is good is simply an added perk. Patrons typically recommend the Choucroute Lipp which is sauerkraut with sausages, pork, and ham. For dessert the Lipp is known for its Millefeuille.

"I'd like him to feel comfortable with us, to feel that he can trust us. I'd like him to tell us how he came to work for Denoyer and to see what he knows about the original painting—where it is, where it's going." He looked at Lucy and smiled. "I'd like him to tell us all the things he shouldn't be telling us."

Lucy frowned. "Do you have a plan?"

"Certainly," said Cyrus. "Get him drunk and hope for the best."

Eiffel Tower, 1913

Me Talk Pretty One Day

BY DAVID SEDARIS (2000)

Born in New York, but raised in Raleigh, North Carolina, David Sedaris has shown how a typical, middle-class upbringing can make for the best humor. After graduating from the Chicago Art Institute in 1987, Sedaris took odd jobs in Chicago, Raleigh, and New York. One evening, after Sedaris read his diary aloud at a club, Ira Glass asked him to read on his radio show, *The Wild*

Room. Sedaris has been reading his diaries aloud and publishing his stories ever since. He now lives in Paris with his partner.

Sedaris is mostly an essayist and humorist. At times his stories are fictitious even though they have his diary-like style filled with his own brand of self-deprecating humor, keen observations, and satirical wit. His career took off with the "Santaland Diaries," an account of working as a Macy's Christmas elf. He writes regularly for *Esquire* and *The New Yorker* and collaborates with his sister, Amy Sedaris, under the name "The Talent Family." He has written a number of plays including *Stump the Host, Stitches, The Book of Liz,* and *One Woman Shoe,* which earned him an Obie Award. National Public Radio distributes his radio performances through *This American Life.*

Me Talk Pretty One Day is a collection of short stories and essays about learning the French language and moving to Paris. The book earned him the 2001 Thurber Prize for American Humor, and the title of "Humorist of the Year" by *Time* magazine. In this essay, "City of Light in the Dark" Sedaris writes about his love of watching American movies in Paris.

"THE CITY OF LIGHT IN THE DARK"

When asked to account for the time I've spent in Paris, I reach for my carton of ticket stubs and groan beneath its weight. I've been here for more than a year, and while I haven't seen the Louvre or the Pantheon, I have seen *The Alamo* and *The Bridge on the River Kwai.* I haven't made it to Versailles but did manage to catch *Oklahoma!, Brazil,* and *Nashville.* Aside from an occasional trip to the flea market, my knowledge of Paris is limited to what I learned in *Gigi.*

THE PANTHÉON

So grateful for his recovery from a terrible illness, King Louis XV vowed to build a great church to honor Saint-Geneviève to replace the one in ruins. Though the foundation was laid in 1758, the church was not completed until 1789, and with the revolution nearing, the church became a panthéon, a place for the tombs of France's finest.

When visitors come from the United States, I draw up little itineraries. "If we go to the three o'clock *Operation Petticoat*, that should give us enough time to make it across town for the six o'clock screening of *It Is Necessary to Save the Soldier Ryan*, unless, of course, you'd rather see the four o'clock *Ruggles of Red Gap* and the seven o'clock *Roman Holiday*. Me, I'm pretty flexible, so why don't *you* decide."

My guests' decisions prove that I am a poor judge of my own character. Ayatollahs are flexible. I am not. Given the choice between four perfectly acceptable movies, they invariably opt for a walk through the Picasso museum or a tour of the cathedral, saying, "I didn't come all the way to Paris so I can sit in the dark."

They make it sound so bad. "Yes," I say, "but this is the French dark. It's . . . darker than the dark we have back home." In the end I give them a map and spare set of keys. They see Notre Dame, I see *The Hunchback of Notre Dame*.

I'm often told that it's wasteful to live in Paris and spend all my time watching American movies, that it's like going to Cairo to eat cheeseburgers. "You could do that back home," people say. But they're wrong. I couldn't live like this in the United States. With very few exceptions, video killed the American revival house. If you want to see a Boris Karloff movie, you have to rent it and watch it on a television set. In Paris it costs as much to rent a movie as it does to go to the theater. French people enjoy going out and watching their movies on a big screen. On any given week one has at least 250 pictures to choose from, at least a third of them in English. There are all the recent American releases, along with any old movie you'd ever want to see. On Easter, having learned that that *The Greatest Story Ever Told* was sold out, I just crossed the street and saw *Superfly*, the second-greatest story ever told. Unless they're for children, all movies are shown in their original English with French subtitles. Someone might say, "Get your fat ass out of here before I do something I regret," and the screen will read, "Leave."

I sometimes wonder why I even bothered with French class. "I am truly delighted to make your acquaintance," "I heartily thank you for this succulent meal"—I have yet to use either of these pleasantries. Since moving to Paris my most often used phrase is, "One place, please." That's what one says at the box office when ordering a ticket, and I say it quite well. In New York I'd go to the movies three or four times a week. Here I've upped it to six or seven, mainly because I'm too lazy to do anything else. Fortunately, going to the movies seems to suddenly qualify as an intellectual accomplishment, on a par with reading a book or devoting time to serious thought. It's not that the movies have gotten any more strenuous, it's just that a lot of people are as lazy as I am, and together we've agreed to lower the bar.

Circumstances foster my laziness. Within a five-block radius of my apartment there are four first-run multiplexes and a dozen thirty-to-fifty-seat revival houses with rotating programs devoted to obscure and well-known actors, directors, and genres. These are the mom-and-pop theaters, willing to proceed with the two o'clock showing of *The Honeymoon Killers* even if I'm the only one in the house. It's as if someone had outfitted his den with a big screen and comfortable chairs. The woman at the box office sells you a ticket, rips it in half, and hands you the stub. Inside the theater you're warmly greeted by a hostess who examines your stub and tears it just enough to make her presence felt. Somewhere along the line someone decided that this activity is worthy of a tip, so you give the woman some change, though I've never known why. It's a mystery, like those big heads on Easter Island or the popularity of the teeny-weeny knapsack.

I'm so grateful such theaters still exist that I'd gladly tip the projectionist as well. Like the restaurants with only three tables, I wonder how some of these places manage to stay open. In America the theaters make most of their money at the concession stand, but here, at least in the smaller places, you'll find nothing but an ice-cream machine tucked away between the bathroom and the fire exit. The larger theaters offer a bit more, but it's still mainly candy and ice cream sold by a vendor with a tray around his neck. American theaters have begun issuing enormous cardboard trays, and it's only a matter of time before the marquees read TRY OUR BARBECUED RIBS! OR COMPLIMENTARY BAKED POTATO WITH EVERY THIRTY-TWO-OUNCE SIRLOIN. When they started selling nachos, I knew that chicken wings couldn't be far behind. Today's hot dogs are only clearing the way for tomorrow's hamburgers, and from there it's only a short leap to the distribution of cutlery.

I've never considered myself an across-the-board apologist for the French, but there's a lot to be said for an entire population that never, under any circumstances, talks during the picture. I've sat through Saturday-night slasher movies with audiences of teenagers and even then nobody has said a word. I can't remember the last time I've enjoyed silence in an American theater. It's easy to believe that our audiences spend the day saying nothing, actually saving their voices for the moment the picture begins. At an average New York screening I once tapped the shoulder of the man in front of me, interrupting his spot review to ask if he planned on talking through the entire movie.

"Well . . . yeah. What about it?" He said this with no trace of shame or apology. It was as if I'd asked if he planned to circulate his blood or draw air into his lungs. "Gee, why wouldn't I?" I moved away from the critic and found myself sitting besides a clairvoyant who loudly predicted the fates of the various characters seen moving their lips up on the screen.

Next came an elderly couple constantly convinced they were missing something. A stranger would knock on the door, and they'd ask, "Who's he?" I wanted to assure them that all their questions would be answered in due time, but I don't believe in talking during movies, so I moved again, hoping I might be lucky enough to find a seat between two people who had either fallen asleep or died.

At a theater in Chicago I once sat beside a man who watched the movie while listening to a Cubs game on his transistor radio. When the usher was called, the sports fan announced that this was a free country and that he wanted to listen to the goddamn game. "Is there a law against doing both things at once?" he asked. "Is there a law? Show me the law, and I'll turn off my radio."

Sitting in Paris and watching my American movies, I think of the man with the transistor radio and feel the exact opposite of homesick. The camera glides over the cities of my past, capturing their energetic skylines just before they're destroyed by the terrorist's bomb or advancing alien warship. New York, Chicago, San Francisco: it's like seeing pictures of people I know I could still sleep with if I wanted to. When the high-speed chases and mandatory shoot-outs become too repetitive, I head over to the revival houses and watch gentler movies in which the couples sleep in separate beds and everyone wears a hat. As my ticket is ripped I'll briefly consider all the constructive things I could be doing. I think of the parks and the restaurants, of the pleasantries I'll never use on the friends I am failing to make. I think of the great city teeming on the other side of that curtain, and then the lights go down, and I love Paris.

Rue de Rivoli, 1906

55 PARIS. — La Rue de Rivoli. — LL.

The Innocents Abroad

BY MARK TWAIN (1869)

In 1835, Samuel Langhorne Clemens was born in the rural town of Florida, Missouri. His family moved to Hannibal, Missouri, where he grew up. At seventeen he moved to St. Louis and worked for a printer while earning his license to become a river pilot. This is when he learned the term "mark twain," meaning that it is safe to navigate. His career as a river pilot was brought to a standstill by the Civil War; so in 1861, he began working for newspapers all across the country and sometimes used the pen name of Mark

Twain. In 1865, his story "The Celebrated Jumping Frog of Calaveras County" appeared in the *New York Saturday Press*, which was the broadest publication he had received to that time. In 1869, he published his first book *The Innocents Abroad*, which was then referred to as travel literature. In 1870 he married Olivia Langdon, and they had four children. In his lifetime, he wrote twenty-eight books along with countless letters and sketches, and short stories. He is most famous for *The Adventures of Tom Sawyer* and *The Adventures of Huckleberry Finn*, the latter is considered one of the greatest American novels. He died in 1910 in his home in Redding, Connecticut.

He was a writer, satirist, and humorist. Four noteworthy traits of Twain's writing style are regional dialect, symbolism, biting sarcasm, and timeless humor. Ernest Hemingway had this to say about Twain's work: "All modern American literature comes from one book by Mark Twain called Huckleberry Finn . . . All American writing comes from that. There was nothing before. There has been nothing as good since."

The Innocents Abroad was written in 1869, five years after Twain had set out on a "world tour," traveling in France and Italy. By weaving wit with descriptions and telling readers what he did not see, hear, or smell, as well as what he did, Twain brought Europe into the homes of Americans who would never have the chance to go abroad. Twain never lost sight of who his readers were nor his own midwestern upbringing. Some of his most famous quotes from his travels were also the most endearing to his American reader: "In Paris, they simply stared when I spoke to them in French; I never did succeed in making those idiots understand their own language." In this portion of *The Innocents Abroad*, Twain and his buddies arrive in France and slowly make their way to Paris. Twain's observations about the contrast between American and French culture have proven timeless on a number of levels.

FROM CHAPTER TWELVE

By Lyons and the Sáone (where we saw the lady of Lyons and thought little of her comeliness), by Villa Franca, Tonnere, venerable Sens, Melun, Fontainebleau, and scores of other beautiful cities, we swept, always noting the absence of hog wallows, broken fences, cow lots, unpainted houses, and mud, and always noting, as well, the presence of cleanliness, grace, taste in adorning and beautifying, even to the disposition of a tree or the turning of a hedge, the marvel of roads in perfect repair, void of ruts and guiltless of even an inequality of surface—we bowled along, hour after hour, that brilliant summer day, and as nightfall approached we entered a wilderness of odorous flowers and shrubbery, sped through it, and then, excited, delighted, and half persuaded that we were only the sport of a beautiful dream, lo, we stood in magnificent Paris!

What excellent order they kept about that vast depot! There was no frantic crowding and jostling, no shouting and swearing, and no swaggering intrusion of services by rowdy hackmen. These latter gentry stood outside—stood quietly by their long line of vehicles and said never a word. A kind of hackman general seemed to have the whole matter of transporation in his hands. He politely received the passengers and ushered them to the kind of conveyance they wanted, and told the driver where to deliver them. There was no "talking back," no dissatisfaction about overcharging, no grumbling about anything. In a little while we were speeding through the streets of Paris and delightfully recognizing certain names and places with which books had long ago made us familiar. It was like meeting an old friend when we read "Rue de Rivoli" on the street corner; we knew the genuine vast palace of the Louvre as well as we knew its picture; when we passed by the Column of July we needed no one to tell us what it was or to remind us that on its site once stood the grim Bastille, that grave of human hopes and happiness, that dismal prison house within whose dungeons so many young faces put on the wrinkles of age, so many proud spirits grew humble, so many brave hearts broke.

RUE DE RIVOLI

This street is named for Napoleon's victory against Austria, at the battle of the Rivoli Gorge in 1797. Napoleon designed the street to face the north wing of the old palace and run directly through the heart of Paris, linking the Louvre and the Champs-Elysées. Today the Rue de Rivoli is as grand as ever and home to some of Paris's finest bookshops, clothing stores, and the famous Hotel de Ville.

We secured rooms at the hotel, or rather, we had three beds put into one room, so that we might be together, and then we went out to a restaurant, just after lamplighting, and ate a comfortable, satisfactory, lingering dinner. It was a pleasure to eat where everything was so tidy, the food so well cooked, the waiters so polite, and the coming and departing company so mustached, so frisky, so affable, so fearfully and wonderfully Frenchy! All the surroundings were gay and enlivening. Two hundred people sat at little tables on the sidewalk, sipping wine and coffee; the streets were thronged with light vehicles and with joyous pleasure-seekers; there was music in the air, life and action all about us, and a conflagration of gaslight everywhere!

After dinner we felt like seeing such Parisian specialties as we might see without distressing exertion, and so we sauntered through the brilliant streets and looked at the dainty trifles in variety stores and jewelry shops. Occasionally, merely for the pleasure of being cruel, we put unoffending Frenchmen on the rack with questions framed in incomprehensible jargon of their native language, and while they writhed we impaled them, we peppered them, we scarified them, with their own vile verbs and participles.

We noticed that in the jewelry stores they had some of the articles marked "gold" and some labeled "imitation." We wondered at this extravagance of honesty and inquired into the matter. We were informed that inasmuch as most people are not able to tell false gold from the genuine article, the government compels jewelers to have their gold work assayed and stamped officially according to its fineness and their imitation work duly labeled with the sign of its falsity. They told us the jewelers would not dare to violate this law, and that whatever a stranger bought in one of their stores might be depended upon as being strictly what it was represented to be. Verily, a wonderful land is France!

* * *

To close our first day in Paris cheerfully and pleasantly, we now sought our grand room in the Grand Hotel du Louvre and climbed into our sumptuous bed and read and smoked—but alas!

It was pitiful,

In a whole city-full,

Gas we had none.

No gas to read by—nothing but dismal candles. It was a shame. We tried to map out excursions for the morrow; we puzzled over French "guides to Paris"; we talked disjointedly in a vain endeavor to make head or tail of the wild chaos of the day's sights and experiences; we subsided to indolent smoking; we gaped and yawned and stretched—then feebly wondered if we were really and truly in renowned Paris, and drifted drowsily away into that vast mysterious void which men call sleep.

FROM CHAPTER THIRTEEN

I am writing this chapter partly for the satisfaction of abusing that accomplished knave Billfinger, and partly to show whosoever shall read this how Americans fare at the hands of the Paris guides and what sort of people Paris guides are. It need not be supposed that we were a stupider or an easier prey than our countrymen generally are, for we were not. The guides deceive and defraud every American who goes to Paris for the first time and sees its sights himself. I shall visit Paris again someday and then let the guides beware! I shall go in my war paint—I shall carry my tomahawk along.

I think we have lost but little time in Paris. We have gone to bed every night tired out. Of course, we visited the renowned International Exposition. All the world did that. We went there on our third day in Paris—and we stayed there *nearly two hours*. That was our first and last visit. To tell the truth, we saw at a glance that one would have to spend weeks—yea, even months—in that monstrous establishment to get an intelligible idea of it.

FROM CHAPTER FOURTEEN

We went to see the Cathedral of Notre Dame.

NOTRE DAME

Perhaps the most famous example of French Gothic architecture, Notre Dame de Paris is both the cathedral of Paris and the seat of the Archbishop. The phrase *notre dame* is French for "our lady" (the Virgin Mary.) During the revolution, much of the church was badly damaged or destroyed; however, the cathedral was restored to its original grandeur in the nineteenth century.

We had heard of it before. It surprises me sometimes to think how much we *do* know and how intelligent we are. We recognized the brown old Gothic pile in a moment; it was like the pictures. We stood at a little distance and gazed long at its stony, mutilated saints who had been looking calmly down from their perches for ages. The Patriarch of Jerusalem stood under them in the old days of chivalry and romance, and preached the third Crusade, more than six hundred years ago; and since that day they have stood there and looked quietly down upon the most thrilling scenes, the grandest pageants, the most extraordinary spectacles that have grieved or delighted Paris. These battered and broken-nosed old fellows saw many and many a cavalcade of mail-clad knights come marching home from Holy Land; they heard the bells above them toll and signal for the St. Bartholomew's Massacre, and they saw the slaughter that followed; later they saw the Reign of Terror, the carnage of the Revolution, the overthrow of a king, the coronation of two Napoleons, the christening of the young prince that lords it over a regiment of servants in the Tuileries today—and they may possibly continue to stand there until they see the Napoleon dynasty swept away and the banners of a great republic floating above its ruins. I wished these old parties could speak. They could tell a tale worth the listening to.

***

One night we went to the celebrated Jardin Mabille, but only stayed a little while.

JARDIN MABILLE

This country dance pavilion opened in 1844, and at the time Twain visited it was the most popular *bal*, as they were called, in the city. Open two or three nights a week in the summer, patrons enjoyed the beautiful garden, comfortable seating, and large dance floor. By 1878, the clientèle had changed. *The New York Times* chronicled the demise of Jardin Mabille in its September 1, 1878, issue. Eventually everything that had once made it grand had faded away until finally it went out of business.

We wanted to see some of this kind of Paris life, however, and therefore the next night we went to a similar place of entertainment in a great garden in the suburb of Asnieres. We went to the railroad depot toward evening, and Ferguson got tickets for a second-class carriage. Such a perfect jam of people I have not often seen—but there was no noise, no disorder, no rowdyism. Some of the women and young girls that entered the train we knew to be of the demimonde, but others we were not at all sure about. The girls and women in our carriage behaved themselves modestly and becomingly all the way out, except that they smoked. When we arrived at the garden in Asnieres, we paid a franc or two admission and entered a place which had flower beds in it, and grass plots and long curving rows of ornamental shrubbery, with here and there a secluded bower convenient for eating ice cream in. We moved along the sinuous gravel walks, with the great concourse of girls and young men, and suddenly a domed and filigreed white temple, starred over and over and over again with brilliant gas jets, burst upon us like a fallen sun. Nearby was a large, handsome house with its ample front illuminated in the same way and above its roof floated the Star-Spangled Banner of America.

"Well!" I said. "How is this?" It nearly took my breath away.

Ferguson said an American—a New Yorker—kept the place, and was carrying on quite a stirring opposition to the Jardin Mabille.

Crowds composed of both sexes and nearly all ages were frisking about the garden or sitting in the open air in front of the flagstaff and the temple, drinking wine and coffee or smoking. The dancing had not begun yet. Ferguson said there was to be an exhibition. The famous Blondin was going to perform on a tightrope in another part of the garden. We went thither. Here the light was dim, and the masses of people were pretty closely packed together. And now I made a mistake which any donkey might make, but a sensible man never. I committed an error which I find myself repeating every day of my life. Standing right before a young lady, I said:

"Dan, just look at this girl, how beautiful she is!"

"I thank you more for the evident sincerity of the compliment, sir, than for the extraordinary publicity you have given to it!" This in good, pure English.

We took a walk, but my spirits were very, very sadly dampened. I did not feel right comfortable for some time afterward. Why will people be so stupid as to suppose themselves the only foreigners among a crowd of ten thousand persons?

But Blondin came out shortly. He appeared on a stretched cable, far away above the sea of tossing hats and handkerchiefs, and in the glare of the hundreds of rockets that whizzed heavenward by him he looked like a wee insect. He balanced his pole and walked the length of his rope—two or three hundred feet; he came back and got a man and carried him across; he returned to the center and danced a jig; next he performed some gymnastic and balancing feats too perilous to afford a pleasant spectacle; and he finished by fastening to his person a thousand Roman candles, Catherine wheels, serpents and rockets of all manner of brilliant colors, setting them on fire all at once and walking and waltzing across his rope again in a blinding blaze of glory that lit up the garden and the people's faces like a great conflagration at midnight.

The dance had begun, and we adjourned to the temple. Within it was a drinking saloon, and all around it was a broad circular platform for the dancers. I backed up against the wall of the temple and waited. Twenty sets formed, the music struck up, and then—I placed my hands before my face for very shame. But I looked through my fingers. They were dancing the renowned "Cancan." A handsome girl in the set before me tripped forward lightly to meet the opposite gentleman, tripped back again, grasped her dresses vigorously on both sides with her hands, raised them pretty high, danced an extraordinary jig that had more activity and exposure about it than any jig I ever saw before, and then drawing her clothes still higher, she advanced gaily to the center and launched a vicious kick full at her vis-a-vis that must infallibly have removed his nose if he had been seven feet high. It was a mercy he was only six.

That is the cancan. The idea of it is to dance as wildly, as noisily, as furiously as you can; expose yourself as much as possible if you are a woman; and kick as high as you can, no matter which sex you belong to. There is no word of exaggeration in this. Any of the staid, respectable, aged people who were there that night can testify to the truth of that statement. There were a good many such people present. I suppose French morality is not of that straight-laced description which is shocked at trifles.

I moved aside and took a general view of the cancan. Shouts, laughter, furious music, a bewildering chaos of darting and intermingling forms, stormy jerking and snatching of gay dresses, bobbing heads, flying arms, lightning flashes of white-stockinged calves and dainty slippers in the air, and then a grand final rush, riot, a terrific hubbub, and a wild stampede! Heavens! Nothing like it has been seen on earth since trembling Tam O'Shanter saw the devil and the witches at their orgies that stormy night in "Alloways auld haunted kirk."

We visited the Louvre, at a time when we had no silk purchases in view, and looked at its miles of paintings by the old masters.

THE MUSÉE DU LOUVRE

Undoubtedly one of the most famous tourist destinations in Paris, the Louvre began as a fortress in 1190 to protect the city against Viking raids. François I transformed the fortress into a palace and as the city grew around the Louvre Louis XIV decided to expand upon the palace even more. The museum has been a part of the Louvre since 1793 and holds one of the most important collections of artwork in the world.

Some of them were beautiful, but at the same time they carried such evidences about them of the cringing spirit of those great men that we found small pleasure in examining them. Their nauseous adulation of princely patrons was more prominent to me and chained my attention more surely than the charms of color and expression which are claimed to be in the pictures. Gratitude for kindnesses is well, but it seems to me that some of those artists carried it so far that it ceased to be gratitude and became worship. If there is a plausible excuse for the worship of men, then by all means let us forgive Rubens and his brethren.

But I will drop the subject, lest I say something about the old masters that might as well be left unsaid.

Of course we drove in the Bois de Boulogne, that limitless park, with its forests, its lakes, its cascades, and its broad avenues. There were thousands upon thousands of vehicles abroad and the scene was full of life and gaiety. There were very common hacks, with father and mother and all the children in them; conspicuous little open carriages with celebrated ladies of questionable reputation in them; there were dukes and duchesses abroad, with gorgeous footmen perched behind, and equally gorgeous outriders perched on each of the six horses; there were blue and silver, and green and gold and pink and black, and all sorts and descriptions of stunning and startling liveries out, and I almost yearned to be a flunky myself, for the sake of the fine clothes.

But presently the Emperor came along and he outshone them all. He was preceded by a bodyguard of gentlemen on horseback in showy uniforms, his carriage horses (there appeared to be somewhere in the remote neighborhood of a thousand of them) were bestridden by gallant-looking fellows, also in stylish uniforms, and after the carriage followed another detachment of bodyguards.

Everybody got out of the way; everybody bowed to the Emperor and his friend the Sultan; and they went by on a swinging trot and disappeared.

I will not describe the Bois de Boulogne. I cannot do it. It is simply a beautiful, cultivated, endless, wonderful wilderness. It is an enchanting place. It is in Paris now, one may say, but a crumbling old cross in one portion of it reminds one that it was not always so. The cross marks the spot where a celebrated troubadour was waylaid and murdered in the fourteenth century. It was in this park that that fellow with the unpronounceable name made the attempt upon the Russian czar's life last spring with a pistol. The bullet struck a tree. Ferguson showed us the place.

Now in America that interesting tree would be chopped down or forgotten within the next five years, but it will be treasured here. The guides will point it out to visitors for the next eight hundred years, and when it decays and falls down they will put up another there and go on with the same old story just the same.

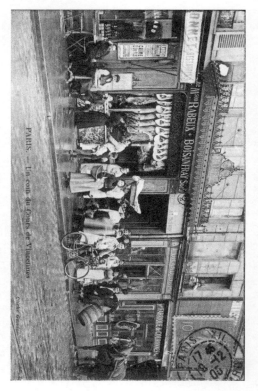

Un Coin du Cours de Vincennes, 1905

April in Paris

BY MICHAEL WALLNER (2006)

Born in Graz, Austria, in 1958, Michael Wallner has worked as an actor, screenwriter, director, and a novelist. He describes his childhood as "ordinary" with a mother who stayed at home and a father who worked in construction (though his parents never married and his father was fifty-six years old when Wallner was born). His father was also an Austrian officer during World War II and spent two of those years in France. Currently, Wallner lives in Germany and divides his time between Berlin and the Black Forest.

His writing is clean and precise, while poetic in both style and pace. He is able to supply just the right amount of character and setting descriptions without interrupting the storyline. Writers such as Mikhail Bulgakov, author of *The Master and Margarita*; William Goldman, who wrote *The Princess Bride*; and Russell Hoban, author of *Kleinzeit*, are among his favorites.

The idea of his debut novel, *April in Paris*, stems from his interest in the phenomenon of living as a stranger among people— especially among people one admires, but who are, at the same time, supposed to be one's enemy. While he uses Paris and World War II as the place and time, Wallner is quick to point out that the story could take place today in Baghdad with a dark skinned American soldier pretending to be an Arab.

The main character of *April in Paris*, Corporal Roth, is a twenty-one-year-old German soldier who speaks French without any trace of an accent. Knowing this, the Gestapo sends him to occupied Paris to translate the confessions of tortured Resistance fighters. Though Roth struggles with the torture he witnesses, he manages to do his job well. Most every night, in an effort to escape his work, he changes into civilian clothing and walks into the streets of Paris where he is flattered to be mistaken for a Frenchman. He introduces himself to people as Antoine and slowly begins to feel at home in Paris surrounded by his enemies. Even more, he grows fond of a young French girl named Chantal, the daughter of a local bookseller.

FROM CHAPTER THREE

The first thing I wanted was a new name, and before I could figure out why and wherefore, I opted for Antoine. Monsieur Antoine, assistant bookseller. I took the small volume out of my pocket: La Fontaine's *Fables*.

LA FONTAINE'S FABLES

Jean de La Fontaine was the most famous French fabulist and among the most widely read French poets in the seventeenth century. His first collection of 124 fables was published in 1668 and dedicated to Louis, le Grand Dauphin, the six-year old son of Louis XIV of France. Flaubert believed that Fontaine was the only French poet to fully master the French language before Victor Hugo.

The book gave me security; it reinforced my biography. Monsieur Antoine, out for a stroll. Only a low-profile promenader, a young man in a check-patterned suit. His footfall sounded the same as that of the people around him. No heavy stepping, no reason for anyone to clear out of his way. I gradually returned to normal breathing and loosened my fearful grip on La Fontaine. I pushed my hat up high on my forehead. For no good reason, I smiled into the late afternoon.

Monsieur Antoine crossed the Pont Royal and turned into the commercial streets near the quays. Fruit and vegetable stands appeared.

THE PONT ROYAL

The Pont Royal links the right bank and the Pavillon de Flore with the left bank of Paris between rue de Bac and rue de Beaunne. In 1685, after years of structural damage, the bridge was rebuilt with stone and five arches. King Louis XIV named it Pont Royal (Napoleon I changed the bridge's name to Pont des Tuileries, but it was quickly changed back after his reign). In the eighteenth century, the bridge was a popular place for festivals. In 2005, Pont Royal was lit up as a part of the Paris Olympic celebration.

Beside them, people were drinking red wine from little glasses. I turned the corner and was immediately surrounded by a babble of voices. Everyone spoke! I heard old men laughing after a girl with a flowered hat passed them. A fat woman shouted across the street, and three other women answered. An abbé, his shoulders gleaming in the bronze-colored light, blinked at a matron and made arcane predictions about the weather. The noisy, chattering world seized me and carried me away into the sounds and the voices. I stopped in front of an old woman with an accordion and tossed a coin into her dish.

"*Que désirez-vous, mon garçon?*" she asked, taking the pipe out of her mouth.

I had resolved to speak as little as possible. Monsieur Antoine, however, found this notion mistaken. On a spring afternoon, a *silent* Parisian would be conspicuous. Everyone around was bustling, boisterous, and abrupt.

There was a song I wanted to hear, a hit, but all I could think of was the refrain: "*Je te veux.*" The old woman nodded appreciatively, stuck the pipe into the corner of her mouth, and began. I listened to her for a while and then walked on. I noticed a lady, a madame, wearing a veil as thin as gossamer; her mouth was painted dark red. A band of teenagers ran past while a cop ambled away in the opposite direction.

I got in line in front of a pastry shop. A small woman crowded me from behind. On the other side of the counter, a skinny shop assistant was tying up packages of cookies. I watched an apprentice, a young girl, furrowing her brow as she read a cheap novel, oblivious to the entire world. I would have been only too happy to know what she found in those words. I got the last remaining package of cookies and paid for it; the small woman gave me dirty looks. I thought about giving her the cookies, but then I laid my book on the package and stuck them both under my arm.

While loitering in front of the shop windows, assuring myself that my suit could pass for a French model, I realized that I had turned into rue de Gaspard.

Today, the narrow street gleamed with a different light. The sinking sun lay deep in the sky, bathing ridges and roofs in warm red. There was no one on the stone in front of the bookshop. I figured it would be senseless to search for the young woman with the cat's face. She'd probably just happened to be there that one time, bought a book, sat on the stone, and read for a while. Then she had gone away, and there was a good chance she'd never return to rue de Gaspard.

The bookshop was closed. Disappointed, I looked up at the name over the portal: JOFFO, LIVRES. Out of curiosity, I tried the door handle. The door opened, and the shop bell rang.

I said in French, "May I come in?"

"Please do, monsieur. Have a look around," the owner replied from behind the counter.

I went to a shelf and stood in such a way that he could see my face. I asked him, "Do you have the new translation of *Anna Karenina*?"

"There's no new translation." The corpulent gentleman shook his head and came closer to me. "At the moment, there's nothing of the sort being published. Prospère has shut down."

Looking the bookseller right in the eyes, I asked to see the old edition. Would he recognize the German corporal who had visited his shop only yesterday?

"This is from before the war," I remarked.

"As I said." He shrugged his shoulders and then noticed the little volume under my arm. "You're reading the *Fables*?" He reached out a hand. "May I?"

I gave him my favorite book.

"This is a rare edition." He smiled the smile of a connoisseur. Fear came over me. Maybe the book bore a German mark of some kind.

Joffo turned to the copyright page. "Look here. This must be the last printing: 1936." He looked at me. "Are you perhaps interested in selling this book?"

"Unfortunately, I can't." I sighed, much relieved. "It was a gift."

"I know I must still have . . ." Much more agile than his bulk suggested, the man dashed over to the next set of shelves and pulled out the fabulous, sumptuously illustrated edition. He showed me the poem called "Fortune and the Young Boy"; the illustration was a full-page engraving by Gustave Doré.

"I used to read from this book to my daughter when she was little," Joffo said.

On the margin of the page, I noticed words scribbled in a childish hand. Suddenly, I seemed to see the butterfly girl, the young woman with the reddish brown hair. My idea was crazy, but I gave it a try. "I haven't seen your daughter at all today."

His head jerked up. His eyes narrowed like a boar's. He said, "Have we met, monsieur?"

"No," I replied with a smile. "But I'm in the neighborhood now and again."

"And your name?"

"Antoine. . . ." My eyes quickly searched book spines. Strings of letters, gold embossing, a curved *r* and *e*, and over there an anthology entitled *Les Barbares*. "Antoine Rebarbes," I said. I took a deep breath.

"You're from Paris?"

"From outside of Paris," I said as calmly as possible. "Will you wrap up the Tolstoy for me?"

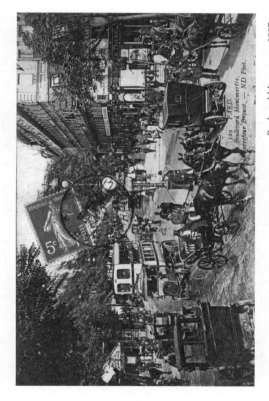

Boulevard Montmartre, 1907

Our Paris

BY EDMUND WHITE (1995)

Edmund White was born in 1940 in Cincinnati, Ohio. His parents divorced when he was seven and he grew up mostly in the Chicago area with his mother. After attending the Cranbrook Academy, White went to the University of Michigan and majored in Chinese. Having dealt with his homosexuality at an early age, White was openly gay when he moved to New York City and he worked for Time-Life Books from 1962 to 1970. He then took a year off to live in Rome. When he returned to New York he became the editor for *The Saturday Review* and *Horizon*. As an aspiring writer living in New York in the 1970s he, along with six other gay men, formed a group of writers and called themselves the Violet Quills.

White published his first novel *Forgetting Elena* in 1973. In 1983, he moved to Paris and lived there for the next seven years. In 1995 he published *Our Paris: Sketches from Memory*. His partner Hubert Sorin did the illustrations.

White is largely known for his work on gay-themed stories, and autobiographical novels in which he is brutally honest about his sexuality. However, not all of his work is centered on gay issues. His novel, *Caracole*, published in 1985, deals with heterosexual relationships and desires, and in 2006 he wrote a play titled *Haute Terre* detailing a fictitious meeting between terrorist Timothy McVeigh and novelist Gore Vidal. No matter the subject, White's writing is smart and precise. He is a keen observer of human emotions and his writing shows a diligence to conveying feelings exactly as they are. His work has earned him high honors including a membership in the American Academy of Arts and Letters as well as the American Academy of Arts and Sciences.

Our Paris: Sketches from Memory is a personal narrative about the author and his gay partner during their years in Paris together. It's lighthearted, yet there is still a personal depth that White manages to achieve in all his work.

FROM CHAPTER TWO

Hubert, like all Frenchmen, takes food very seriously and likes it fresh, so I go shopping every day on the rue Rambuteau, in the shadow of the Centre Georges Pompidou.

THE POMPIDOU CENTER

This institution was named after President Georges Pompidou who wanted to create a place that was not only dedicated to modern art, but was itself a modern, innovative creation. A pair of young architects from Italy and Great Britain won a contest for designing the most innovative building. The building frees up the interior by having all the workings of the building exposed on the exterior.

This street runs through the no-man's-land between Les Halles (a faceless, modern shopping district, much of it below ground) and the upscale area of the Marais, the heart of aristocratic Paris in the seventeenth century and now the closest thing to a gay ghetto to be found in France.

THE MARAIS

In the seventeenth century the aristocracy took to building outlandish homes in the Marais, but during the Revolution they abandoned these palaces for safer places in Versailles. The area quickly fell to ruins and there seemed to be little hope for it until Jews from Eastern Europe began moving into the area in the late nineteenth century. This first wave of progress, however, was cut short by World War II. Even after the Second World War ended, the Marais continued to decline until 1969 when the area became the city's first protected sector—an area where incentives are given for revitalization.

Despite the chic museum landmark, Rambuteau couldn't be more typically French (France, don't forget, is a country where the people spend a quarter of their income on food). There *is* a small supermarket, but since I'm always with Fred and he's not welcome,

I avoid it. All the other stores either open onto the street or are actually in it, like the little old flower man with his cart.

First Fred and I go to the fish man, who drives me mad because he insists on speaking English. Not that he knows anything *useful* in English, such as the names of fish or pounds instead of kilos. In a weak moment he once confessed to me that he hates the English (that was after he found out I was American), but then when the trade talks were going badly with the Americans and irate French fishermen were throwing their catch back in the ocean just to spite everyone, he announced he hated Americans, too, and was boycotting Euro Disney. He preferred to take his kids to something educational, such as that theme park outside Paris devoted entirely to scale models of important French châteaux. Not my idea of a fun family outing, but the French can't enjoy themselves if they don't think they're learning something. Ever notice how they crowd in front of the long, written explanations at the beginning of a museum show and whiz past the paintings themselves?

But he does have nice fish, and in the best French didactic manner he'll even write out recipes for me if I ask him. There he reverts to his native language and uses lovely expressions such as "a tear of wine" (*une larme de vin*), "a suspicion of ginger" (*un soupçon de gingembre*), "a cloud of milk" (*un nuage de lait*) or "a nut of butter" (*une noix de beurre*). The best recipe he gave me was for mussels: "Brown two chopped onions and a piece of garlic in a thread of butter, then when they're transparent add two cups of dry white wine and a cup of water, salt and pepper, and a bay leaf. Let them bubble nicely while you clean a quart of mussels for each person. With your fingers pull off the beard (it rips off easily if you're pulling in the right direction). Throw away the mussels that are open when uncooked. Now put the good mussels in a casserole, cover with a lid, after five minutes shake them well to change their position and in five more minutes lift them out with a slotted spoon onto a waiting dish with a cover and pour the juice through a strainer lined with cheesecloth to remove the remaining grains of sand. Serve with a baguette for a hearty first course."

FROM CHAPTER TEN

Our neighborhood, the Châtelet, is characterless by day, more a corridor between the shops and restaurants of Les Halles and the boutiques and bistros of the Marais than a proper place of its own. At night, however, it resumes its identity as one of the oldest parts of Paris.

THE MARAIS TODAY

If you visit the Marais today you will be welcomed with quaint narrow passageways that are bustling with galleries and boutiques. (One street of note is the rue des Francs-Bourgeois, as it is one of the few streets in Paris where all the shops are open on Sunday.) There is a mix of Jewish, Algerian, and Asian settlers and since the mid 1980s, the southwestern portion of the Marais has become the center of the gay community.

Our street, the rue St.-Martin, for instance, was built by the Romans as their main north-south route. The next street over, the rue Quincampoix, is just the width of a car, and at least in the stretch near our house, the huge seventeenth century doors, lacquered teal blue or just treated with clear varnish to show the natural wood, lead into narrow courtyards and dark stairways.

Often when I go out at night with Fred we collide with the guys carrying into Mona Lisa it the books they display on the sidewalk by day, and I run into a thin woman with white hair who I'd guess is close to seventy except she likes to run in sneakers—she says in order to tire her small, excitable puppy, Trompette. When she's not running she'll stroll beside us while Trompette runs circles around Fred, who looks both smiling and sad, as though he'd love to play, if only she'd slow down to a proper, stately basset rhythm.

Trompette's owner tells me she's lived in the Châtelet all her life and before she retired she was an usher (*une ouvreuse*) at the Théâtre Musical de Paris (which everyone calls just "the Châtelet") when it performed fun operettas and musical comedies, before it turned to grand opera (such as the current Wagner cycle) and symphony concerts. She recalls that when Les Halles was still the food market of Paris, even the rue St.-Martin was stacked high with rabbit cages and cartons of vegetables. She points out a walled-up building on the rue des Lombards where, she says, a theater troupe of squatters performed until just recently. "It was really *sympathique*. They even had performances for children on Wednesday afternoons; I'd bring my grandniece. No electricity, of course, so they acted by candle-light. You paid what you could, and even if you gave them nothing at all they didn't grumble. Naturally, an easygoing, utopian group like that has no way of keeping out the bad element, so soon there were drug addicts and even thieves, and the fire department closed them down and had the window and doors bricked in, though they say a few hoboes still live in there. They must have a tunnel in."

* * *

The Châtelet is the very heart of Paris, a bit like what Piccadilly Circus is to London or Times Square is to New York. At one corner of the neighborhood is the Centre Georges Pompidou, that massive oil refinery posing as a museum of modern art.

THE POMPIDOU CENTER TODAY

The Center opened in 1977 and is visited by more than six million people each year. Perhaps its most distinguishing factor, other than its exterior appearance, is the notable collection of modern and contemporary European art it holds. The Center also has a large public library, a cinema, a music research institute, bookstores, and cafés.

When Hubert and I met Richard Rogers, the architect, in London, I said, "Oh, we live just next door to your museum," and he said, "And it's not rusting." I never liked the museum before I met him, but he was so charming and his American wife, Ruthie, gave us such a great meal at her restaurant, the River Café, right next to the Thames, and Hubert was so starry-eyed about meeting such a great architect (did I mention that Hubert is an architect?)—that now of course I love the museum. When I used to object to it, Parisian friends would say, "Edmund, you're like those people who objected to the Eiffel Tower." My main quibble in the old days before we met Richard Rogers was that it was rusting, but now of course I've learned not to say that. It appears the whole museum is being shut down for major repairs, which are needed in part because of the volume of visitors—*much* heavier than anyone ever anticipated.

It attracts busloads of tourists from Germany, Holland, England, and now even from Hungary, the Czech Republic and Poland. If the Pompidou draws more tourists than any other French monument, including the Eiffel Tower, that's because it's free—at least the escalator ride to the top is free. Also free are the ground-floor exhibits and stores and the library—where you can roam through the open stacks (quite a rarity in France). Of course you have to pay to get into the upstairs galleries, but few people brave them. For the cost of a coffee you can sit at a table and look in one direction up to the heights of Montmartre, where the pale dome of Sacré-Coeur glows against the sky like the Taj Mahal; or west to the upended hairpin of the Eiffel Tower; or south to the twin square towers of Notre-Dame and, beyond, to the hideous Montparnasse Tower.

THE SACRÉ-COEUR

This church was the idea of two men who promised to build a place that would honor the sacred heart of Christ if Paris was spared an invasion during the Prussian War. Construction began in 1875 and was completed in 1914. Émile Zola was highly critical of this monument in his book, *Paris*, published in 1896. However, his words were practically unnoticed since the public was in favor of the temple.

Les Halles, 1907

The Fat and the Thin

BY ÉMILE ZOLA (1873)

Born in Paris in 1840, Émile Zola was raised in Aix-en-Provence. His family was poor and his father died when he was only seven. He and his mother moved to Paris and he became close friends with artist Paul Cézanne. He published his first set of short stories in 1864, then went on to write his breakthrough novel *Therese Raquin*. Both controversial and political, Zola used his talents and persuasion as a writer to fight injustices as he saw them; thereby making as many enemies as friends. He died in his home in 1902 from poisonous fumes from his blocked chimney, and some have speculated that he was murdered by those who wanted him quieted.

Perhaps the best novelist in the world during the last half of the nineteenth century, Zola took realism farther than other writers had at that point. That is, he mastered the art of writing about life without any idealization or romanticism. His greatest literary feat was a long series of novels, twenty books, titled *La Bête Humaine* (The Beast in Man), published in 1890. The books are set in Paris and deal with everything from the impoverished to the imperial courts. In 1877, his depiction of alcoholism struck a chord with readers making his name known to all of France. He wrote *Le Ventre de Paris* later in life and it is considered one of his most well-written and powerful pieces of work.

Le Ventre de Paris was translated into English by Ernest Alfred Vizetelly in 1888 and titled *The Fat and the Thin*. Since then some revisions have been made to Vizetelly's translation and it has been renamed *The Belly of Paris*; however, this excerpt comes directly from the 1888 translation. The novel is not well-known in America, but it is an outstanding and memorable work even by Zola's standards. The narrator, Florent Quenu, who escaped Devil's Island where he was unjustly held prisoner following Louis-Napoléon's coup-d'etat, has finally returned to Paris to find that the city has changed dramatically. Through Florent's experiences, Zola juxtaposes the two sides of Paris using food as his focal point, with those who have it in abundance surrounding others who are starving.

FROM CHAPTER ONE

When he at length reached Courbevoie, the night was very dark. Paris, looking like a patch of star-spread sky that had fallen upon the black earth, seemed to him to wear a forbidding aspect, as though angry at his return. Then he felt very faint, and his legs almost gave way beneath him as he descended the hill. As he crossed the Neuilly bridge he sustained himself by clinging to the parapet, and bent over and looked at the Seine rolling inky waves between its dense, massy banks.

THE NEUILLY BRIDGE

The area surrounding the Pont du Neuilly dates back to 1222 when a small settlement was recorded in the charter of the Abbey of Saint-Denis as Neuilly (though the ancient origins of the name are still debated). During the Revolution, the settlement was referred to as Port-Neuilly, and in 1897 the commune changed its name to Neuilly-sur-Seine. Today, this community is home to France's most affluent citizens, and the Pont du Neuilly is a station on Line One of the Metro.

A red lamp on the water seemed to be watching him with a sanguineous eye. And then he had to climb the hill if he would reach Paris on its summit yonder. The hundreds of leagues which he had already travelled were as nothing to it. That bit of a road filled him with despair. He would never be able, he thought, to reach yonder light crowned summit. The spacious avenue lay before him with its silence and its darkness, its lines of tall trees and low houses, its broad grey footwalks, speckled with the shadows of overhanging branches, and parted occasionally by the gloomy gaps of side streets. The squat yellow flames of the gas lamps, standing erect at regular intervals, alone imparted a little life to the lonely wilderness. And Florent seemed to make no progress; the avenue appeared to grow ever longer and longer, to be carrying Paris away into the far depths of the night. At last he fancied that the gas lamps, with their single eyes, were running off on either hand, whisking the road away with them; and then, overcome by vertigo, he stumbled and fell on the roadway like a log.

Now he was lying at ease on his couch of greenery, which seemed to him soft as a feather bed. He had slightly raised his head so as to keep his eyes on the luminous haze which was spreading above the dark roofs which he could divine on the horizon. He was nearing his goal, carried along towards it, with nothing to do but to yield to the leisurely jolts of the waggon; and, free from all further fatigue, he now only suffered from hunger. Hunger, indeed, had once more awoke within him with frightful and well nigh intolerable pangs. His limbs seemed to have fallen asleep; he was only conscious of the existence of his stomach, horribly cramped and twisted as by a red-hot iron. The fresh odour of the vegetables, amongst which he was lying, affected him so keenly that he almost fainted away. He strained himself against that piled-up mass of food with all his remaining strength, in order to compress his stomach and silence its groans. And the nine other waggons behind him, with their mountains of cabbages and peas, their piles of artichokes, lettuces, celery, and leeks, seemed to him to be slowly overtaking him, as though to bury him whilst he was thus tortured by hunger beneath an avalanche of food.

Presently the procession halted, and there was a sound of deep voices. They had reached the barriers, and the municipal customs officers were examining the waggons. A moment later Florent entered Paris, in a swoon, lying atop of the carrots, with clenched teeth.

"Hallow! You up there!" Madame François called out sharply.

And as the stranger made no attempt to move, she clambered up and shook him. Florent rose to a sitting posture. He had slept and no longer felt the pangs of hunger, but was dizzy and confused.

"You'll help me to unload, won't you?" Madame François said to him, as she made him get down. He helped her. A stout man with a felt hat on his head and a badge in the top buttonhole of his coat was striking the ground with a stick and grumbling loudly:

"Come, come, now, make haste! You must get on faster than that! Bring the waggon a little more forward. How many yards' standing have you? Four, isn't it?"

Then he gave a ticket to Madame François, who took some coppers out of a little canvas bag and handed them to him; whereupon he went off to vent his impatience and tap the ground with his stick a little further away. Madame François took hold of Balthazar's bridle and backed him so as to bring the wheels of the waggon close to the footway. Then, having marked out her four yards with some wisps of straw, after removing the back of the cart, she asked Florent to hand her the vegetables bunch by bunch. She arranged them sort by sort on her standing, setting them out artistically, the "tops" forming a band of greenery around each pile; and it was with remarkable rapidity that she completed her show, which, in the gloom of early morning, looked like some piece of symmetrically coloured tapestry. When Florent had handed her a huge bunch of parsley, which he had found at the bottom of the cart, she asked him for still another service.

"It would be very kind of you," said she, "if you would look after my goods while I put the horse and cart up. I'm only going a couple of yards, to the Golden Compasses, in the Rue Montorgueil."

Florent told her that she might make herself easy. He preferred to remain still, for his hunger had revived since he had begun to move about. He sat down and leaned against a heap of cabbages beside Madame François's stock. He was all right there, he told himself, and would not go further afield, but wait. His head felt empty, and he had no very clear notion as to where he was. At the beginning of September it is quite dark in the early morning. Around him lighted lanterns were flitting or standing stationary in the depths of the gloom. He was sitting on one side of a broad street which he did not recognise; it stretched far away into the blackness of the night. He could make out nothing plainly, excepting the stock of which he had been left in charge. All around him along the market footways rose similar piles of goods. The middle of the roadway was blocked by huge grey tumbrels, and from one end of the street to the other a sound of heavy breathing passed, betokening the presence of horses which the eye could not distinguish.

Shouts and calls, the noise of falling wood, or of iron chains slipping to the ground, the heavy thud of loads of vegetables discharged from the waggons, and the grating of wheels as the carts were backed against the footways, filled the yet sonorous awakening, whose near approach could be felt and heard in the throbbing gloom. Glancing over the pile of cabbages behind him, Florent caught sight of a man wrapped like a parcel in his cloak, and snoring away with his head upon some baskets of plums. Nearer to him, on his left, he could distinguish a lad, some ten years old, slumbering between two heaps of endive, with an angelic smile on his face. And as yet there seemed to be nothing on that pavement that was really awake except the lanterns waving from invisible arms, and flitting and skipping over the sleep of the vegetables and human beings spread out there in heaps pending the dawn. However, what surprised Florent was the sight of some huge pavilions on either side of the street, pavilions with lofty roofs that seemed to expand and soar out of sight amidst a swarm of gleams. In his weakened state of mind he fancied he beheld a series of enormous, symmetrically built palaces, light and airy as crystal, whose fronts sparkled with countless streaks of light filtering through endless Venetian shutters. Gleaming between the slender pillar shafts these narrow golden bars seemed like ladders of light mounting to the gloomy line of the lower roofs, and then soaring aloft till they reached the jumble of higher ones, thus describing the open framework of immense square halls, where in the yellow flare of the gas lights a multitude of vague, grey, slumbering things was gathered together.

At last Florent turned his head to look about him, distressed at not knowing where he was, and filled with vague uneasiness by the sight of that huge and seemingly fragile vision. And now, as he raised his eyes, he caught sight of the luminous dial and the grey massive pile of Saint Eustache's Church. At this he was much astonished. He was close to Saint Eustache, yet all was novel to him.

THE SAINT EUSTACHE CHURCH

Built between 1532 and 1632, the Saint Eustache was never completed, so it has a rather odd look about it. Nonetheless, it was once considered the church of royalty since it was close to the Royal Palace at the

Louvre. Mozart's mother's funeral was held in the church and King Louis XIV also took communion here. Organ concert recitals are given in the church during the summer months.

However, Madame François had come back again, and was engaged in a heated discussion with a man who carried a sack over his shoulder and offered to buy her carrots for a sou a bunch.

"Really, now, you are unreasonable, Lacaille!" said she. "You know quite well that you will sell them again to the Parisians at four and five sous the bunch. Don't tell me that you won't! You may have them for two sous the bunch, if you like."

Then, as the man went off, she continued: "Upon my word, I believe some people think that things grow of their own accord! Let him go and find carrots at a sou the bunch elsewhere, tipsy scoundrel that he is! He'll come back again presently, you'll see."

These last remarks were addressed to Florent. And, seating herself by his side, Madame François resumed: "If you've been a long time away from Paris, you perhaps don't know the new markets. They haven't been built for more than five years at the most. That pavilion you see there beside us is the flower and fruit market. The fish and poultry markets are farther away, and over there behind us come the vegetables and the butter and cheese. There are six pavilions on this side, and on the other side, across the road, there are four more, with the meat and the tripe stalls. It's an enormous place, but it's horribly cold in the winter. They talk about pulling down the houses near the corn market to make room for two more pavilions. But perhaps you know all this?"

"No, indeed," replied Florent; "I've been abroad. And what's the name of that big street in front of us?"

"Oh, that's a new street. It's called the Rue du Pont Neuf. It leads from the Seine through here to the Rue Montmartre and the Rue Montorgueil. You would soon have recognized where you were if it had been daylight."

RUE MONTORGUEIL

One of Paris's oldest streets, the rue Montorgueil is in the Châtelet-Les Halles District and filled with well-known restaurants, cafés, bakeries, cheese, wine, and flower shops. At the south end of the street sits the famous Saint Eustache Church and Les Halles; the north end has the Grands Boulevards.

Madame François paused and rose, for she saw a woman heading down to examine her turnips. "Ah, is that you, Mother Chantemesse?" she said in a friendly way.

Florent meanwhile glanced towards the Rue Montorgueil. It was there that a body of police officers had arrested him on the night of December 4. He had been walking along the Boulevard Montmartre at about two o'clock, quietly making his way through the crowd, and smiling at the number of soldiers that the Elysee had sent into the streets to awe the people, when the military suddenly began making a clean sweep of the thoroughfare, shooting folks down at close range during a quarter of an hour. Jostled and knocked to the ground, Florent fell at the corner of the Rue Vivienne and knew nothing further of what happened, for the panic-stricken crowd, in their wild terror of being shot, trampled over his body. Presently, hearing everything quiet, he made an attempt to rise; but across him there lay a young woman in a pink bonnet, whose shawl had slipped aside, allowing her chemisette, pleated in little tucks, to be seen. Two bullets had pierced the upper part of her bosom; and when Florent gently removed the poor creature to free his legs, two streamlets of blood oozed from her wounds on to his hands. Then he sprang up with a sudden bound, and rushed madly away, hatless and with his hands still wet with blood. Until evening he wandered about the streets, with his head swimming, ever seeing the young woman lying across his legs with her pale face, her blue staring eyes, her distorted lips, and her expression of astonishment at thus meeting death so suddenly. He was a shy, timid fellow. Albeit thirty years old he had never dared to stare women in the face; and now, for the rest of his life, he was to have that one fixed in his heart and memory. He felt as though he had lost some loved one of his own.

In the evening, without knowing how he had got there, still dazed and horrified as he was by the terrible scenes of the afternoon, he had found himself at a wine shop in the Rue Montorgueil, where several men were drinking and talking of throwing up barricades. He went away with them, helped them to tear up a few paving-stones, and seated himself on the barricade, weary with his long wandering through the streets, and reflecting that he would fight when the soldiers came up. However, he had not even a knife with him, and was still bareheaded. Towards eleven o'clock he dozed off, and in his sleep could see the two holes in the dead woman's white chemisette glaring at him like eyes reddened by tears and blood. When he awoke he found himself in the grasp of four police officers, who were pummelling him with their fists. The men who had built the barricade had fled. The police officers treated him with still greater violence, and indeed almost strangled him when they noticed that his hands were stained with blood. It was the blood of the young woman.

Florent raised his eyes to the luminous dial of Saint Eustache with his mind so full of these recollections that he did not notice the position of the pointers. It was, however, nearly four o'clock. The markets were as yet wrapped in sleep. Madame François was still talking to old Madame Chantemesse, both standing and arguing about the price of turnips, and Florent now called to mind how narrowly he had escaped being shot over yonder by the wall of Saint Eustache. A detachment of gendarmes had just blown out the brains of five unhappy fellows caught at a barricade in the Rue Greneta. The five corpses were lying on the footway, at a spot where he thought he could now distinguish a heap of rosy radishes. He himself had escaped being shot merely because the policemen only carried swords. They took him to a neighbouring police station and gave the officer in charge a scrap of paper, on which were these words written in pencil: "Taken with blood-stained hands. Very dangerous." Then he had been dragged from station to station till the morning came. The scrap of paper accompanied him wherever he went. He was manacled and guarded as though he were a raving madman. At the station in the Rue de la Lingerie some tipsy soldiers wanted to shoot him; and they had already lighted a lantern with that object when the order arrived for the prisoners to be taken to the depot of the Prefecture of Police. Two days afterwards he found himself in a casemate of the fort of Bicêtre. Ever since then he had been suffering from hunger. He had felt hungry in the casemate, and the pangs of hunger had never since left him. A hundred men were pent in the depths of that cellar-like dungeon, where, scarce able to breathe, they devoured the few mouthfuls of bread that were thrown to them, like so many captive wild beasts.

When Florent was brought before an investigating magistrate, without anyone to defend him, and without any evidence being adduced, he was accused of belonging to a secret society; and when he swore that this was untrue, the magistrate produced the scrap of paper from amongst the documents before him: "Taken with blood-stained hands. Very dangerous." That was quite sufficient. He was condemned to transportation. Six weeks afterwards, one January night, a gaoler awoke him and locked him up in a court-yard with more than four hundred other prisoners. An hour later this first detachment started for the pontoons and exile, hand-cuffed and guarded by a double file of gendarmes with loaded muskets. They crossed the Austerlitz bridge, followed the line of the boulevards, and so reached the terminus of the Western Rail-way line. It was a joyous carnival night. The windows of the res-taurants on the boulevards glittered with lights. At the top of the Rue Vivienne, just at the spot where he ever saw the young woman lying dead—that unknown young woman whose image he always bore with him—he now beheld a large carriage in which a party of masked women, with bare shoulders and laughing voices, were venting their impatience at being detained, and expressing their horror of that endless procession of convicts. The whole of the way from Paris to Havre the prisoners never received a mouthful of bread or a drink of water. The officials had forgotten to give them their rations before starting, and it was not till thirty-six hours afterwards, when they had been stowed away in the hold of the frigate *Canada*, that they at last broke their fast.

No, Florent had never again been free from hunger. He recalled all the past to mind, but could not recollect a single hour of satiety. He had become dry and withered; his stomach seemed to have shrunk; his skin clung to his bones. And now that he was back in Paris once more, he found it fat and sleek and flourishing, teem-ing with food in the midst of the darkness. He had returned to it on a couch of vegetables; he lingered in its midst encompassed by unknown masses of food which still and ever increased and disquieted him. Had that happy carnival night continued throughout those seven years, then? Once again he saw the glittering windows on the boulevards, the laughing women, the luxurious, greedy city which he had quitted on that far-away January night; and it seemed to him that everything had expanded and increased in harmony with those huge markets, whose gigantic breathing, still heavy from the indigestion of the previous day, he now began to hear.

Index

ABOUT THE AUTHOR

Jamie Cox Robertson holds a Masters in Literature and lectures at Suffolk University. She lives in Boston with her husband Christopher and daughter Sophia.